FIFTY PLACES TO DRINK

BEER

BEFORE YOU DIE

**Beer Experts Share
the World's Greatest Destinations**

Chris Santella

FOREWORD BY JIM KOCH

ABRAMS IMAGE

NEW YORK

This book is for all of my friends with whom I've enjoyed a pint or two . . .
and for Cassidy, Annabel, and Deidre, who always say, "Have fun!"
when I ask if it's okay to pop out for a beer.

ALSO BY THE AUTHOR

Fifty Places to Camp Before You Die:
Camping Experts Share the World's Greatest Destinations

Fifty Places to Paddle Before You Die:
Kayaking and Rafting Experts Share the World's Greatest Destinations

Fifty Places to Bike Before You Die:
Biking Experts Share the World's Greatest Destinations

Fifty Places to Fly Fish Before You Die:
Fly-Fishing Experts Share the World's Greatest Destinations

Fifty More Places to Fly Fish Before You Die:
Fly-Fishing Experts Share More of the World's Greatest Destinations

Fifty Places to Ski & Snowboard Before You Die:
Downhill Experts Share the World's Greatest Destinations

Fifty Places to Sail Before You Die:
Sailing Experts Share the World's Greatest Destinations

Fifty Places to Go Birding Before You Die:
Birding Experts Share the World's Greatest Destinations

Fifty Places to Dive Before You Die:
Diving Experts Share the World's Greatest Destinations

Fifty Places to Hike Before You Die:
Outdoor Experts Share the World's Greatest Destinations

Fifty Places to Play Golf Before You Die:
Golf Experts Share the World's Greatest Destinations

Fifty More Places to Play Golf Before You Die:
Golf Experts Share the World's Greatest Destinations

Once in a Lifetime Trips:
The World's Fifty Most Extraordinary and Memorable Travel Experiences

Fifty Favorite Fly-Fishing Tales:
Expert Fly Anglers Share Stories from the Sea and Stream

Why I Fly Fish:
Passionate Anglers on the Pastime's Appeal and How It Has Shaped Their Lives

The Hatch Is On!

The Tug is the Drug

CAT WARS (with Dr. Peter Marra)

Contents

ACKNOWLEDGMENTS

This book would not have been possible without the generous assistance of the beer enthusiasts—brewers, impresarios, writers, and aficionados—who shared their time and palates to help bring these fifty great beer-drinking venues to life. To these men and women, I offer the most heartfelt thanks. I also wish to acknowledge the fine efforts of my agent, Stephanie Kip Rostan; my editors, Samantha Weiner and Gabriel Levinson; designer Anna Christian; and copy editor David Blatty, who all helped to bring the book into being. There's not space enough to raise a pint to all the friends who I've been fortunate enough to share good times with over the years, but a few include Pete Marra, Dave Sinise, Howard Kyser, Jerry Stein, Mike McDonough, Ed O'Brien, Andy and Peter Waugh, Chris Bittenbender, Dave Tegeler, Don Ryder, Jake Appelsmith, Chris Lande, Peter Clough, Geoff Roach, Peter Gyerko, Ken Matsumoto, Joe Runyon, Mark Harrison, Jeff Sang, Mike Christensen, Nelson Mathews, Dave Moskowitz, Kenton Quist, Gary Smith, Mike Marcus, Sloan Morris, Doug Mateer, Keith Carlson, Doug Levin, Kirk Deeter, and Greg Thomas. Finally, I want to extend a special thanks to my wife, Deidre, and my daughters, Cassidy and Annabel, who are ever so patient with my travel and deadlines . . . and to my parents, Tina and Andy Santella, who have not likely ever tasted an IPA but have always encouraged me to pursue my passions.

OPPOSITE:
During Oktoberfest, 6.4 million attendees drink 1.8 billion gallons of beer.

FOREWORD

Fifty Places to Drink Beer Before You Die is a book whose time has come! When I started brewing Samuel Adams in 1984, there were only about fifty breweries operating in the United States. Today, more than four thousand independent craft breweries are thriving here. The craft beer renaissance has not been limited to the U.S., however. Innovative craft breweries have sprung up all over the world. This is the greatest time in history to be a beer lover!

Reading this book will inspire you to grab two things: your favorite beer and your suitcase. What a wonderful quest to map out all the places where you've had a beer or would like to have a beer.

An unforgettable beer experience has many elements. Certainly, the quality of the beer is critical, but it's also the place. Back in 1992 I went to Argentina to climb Aconcagua, the highest mountain in the western hemisphere. I brought a bottle of Sam Adams with me and strapped it to my body to keep it from freezing. When we reached the summit, I pulled it out from my climbing clothing and opened it. Thanks to the twenty-three-thousand foot altitude, the beer quickly erupted into a foamy geyser, and I got only a small sip of my Boston Lager. Still, it's one of the top fifty places I've ever enjoyed a beer in my life, aside, of course, from our Boston brewery.

I've always thought there is special magic in the first sip of a wonderful beer. Aaaah! If you combine the magic of the first sip with a magic moment, that's as good as it gets.

So, as you travel the world seeking peak beer experiences, don't forget to seek life's peak moments as well. Nothing goes better with a great beer than a memorable experience with family, friends, and the people you meet while traveling in pursuit of the best beer experience.

Cheers!

—JIM KOCH, FOUNDER OF BOSTON BEER COMPANY
   AND BREWER OF SAMUEL ADAMS

INTRODUCTION

When I came of legal drinking age in 1981, Budweiser was still truly the king of beers. During my college years, I must admit that I enjoyed more than my share. (On a special night, my motley college crew might spring for Michelob or Molson Golden.) After graduation, I took a cross-country road trip with some buddies and landed in San Francisco. There, someone handed me an Anchor Steam—the first craft beer that had ever passed my lips. I can't say that I appreciated it at the time. But it showed me that beer could have, well, flavor. This was confirmed again the next year during a trip to England. By the time I moved to San Francisco in 1990, the first salvos of the microbrewery revolution were being launched all around the country. Soon, I had bid farewell to American lagers and hitched the fortunes of my ever-expanding waistline to steam beers and pale ales, porters and IPAs.

I wrote *Fifty Places to Drink Beer Before You Die* for people like me who appreciate a good pint and all the camaraderie that can come with it.

"What makes a destination a place where you have to drink beer before you die?" you might ask. A city with a rich and influential brewing history? A community that's embraced craft brewing and has attracted other like-minded souls and made it their own? The availability of a celebrated brew that's simply not distributed anywhere else? Or a special setting—be it a renowned nineteenth hole or celebrated lodge—where a cold beer allows a chance to recount a special day? The answer would be yes to all of the above and an abundance of other criteria. One thing I knew when I began this project: I could not assemble this list alone. So I followed a recipe that's served me well in my first twelve Fifty Places books—to seek the advice of some experts. To write *Fifty Places to Drink Beer Before You Die*, I interviewed a host of people closely connected with the brewing world (and several aficionados associated with other areas of endeavor) to discuss some of their favorite spots and experiences. These experts range from craft brewing pioneers (like Jim Koch, Steve Hindy, and Gary Fish) to celebrated beer writers (like Don "Joe Sixpack" Russell, Joe Wiebe, and John Foyston) to professional athletes (like Tommy Moe and Terry Simms). Some spoke of venues that are near and dear to their hearts, places where they've built their professional reputation; others spoke of places they've only visited once but that made a profound impression. To give a sense of the breadth of

the interviewees' backgrounds, a bio of each individual is included after each essay. ("Places," in this context, does not generally reference specific pubs or breweries, but to regions that have a thriving craft beer culture or are celebrated for activities that are nicely complemented by a good beer.)

Wonderful beer-drinking venues can take many shapes and forms. For some, it may be a cool, drizzly city with a host of snug pubs serving British-style ales by a crackling fire; for others, it could be a sun-drenched festival where one can sample hundreds of beers with tens of thousands of like-minded folk. While *Fifty Places to Drink Beer Before You Die* attempts to capture the spectrum of experiences, it by no means attempts to rank the places discussed. Such ranking is, of course, largely subjective.

In the hope that a few readers might embark on their own beer-tasting adventures, brief "If You Go" information is provided at the end of each chapter, including phone numbers/websites of some recommended breweries/brewpubs/pubs in the region described. The "If You Go" information is by no means a comprehensive list, but should give would-be travelers a starting point for planning their trip. (Many pubs and breweries have an active social media presence and will regularly provide updates on what beers are pouring and what's coming down the pipeline.)

Thanks to the incredible proliferation of craft breweries the world has seen in the last ten years, one no longer needs to travel to Germany to find a decent Weissbier or Oregon to imbibe a hop-heavy IPA. Yet a trip to any of the "beervanas" discussed here can create memories for a lifetime. It's my hope that this little book will inspire you to embark on some new tasting adventures of your own.

Craft beer is about quality, not quantity. I encourage you to drink responsibly.
If you do enjoy a few, please don't drive.

OPPOSITE:
Allagash Brewing in Portland, Maine, has built a reputation for its Belgian-inspired ales.
NEXT PAGE:
The deck at Nihiwatu on the island of Sumba is the perfect place to enjoy a Bintang, Indonesia's most popular beer.

The Destinations

BIRMINGHAM

RECOMMENDED BY **Stuart Carter**

The craft-brewing revolution was a bit slow to arrive in Alabama. It's no small wonder that it arrived at all.

"I arrived in Birmingham in the fall of 2005," Stuart Carter recalled. "When I went to the store to check out the beer section, my first reaction was, 'Where is the beer?' I saw all the mass brands, but not much else. One day I was grousing to a colleague about the lack of good beer. He explained the state of affairs in Alabama. At that point, beer stronger than 6 percent ABV was illegal in the state of Alabama. And beer couldn't be sold in sizes above sixteen ounces. My colleague also told me about Free the Hops, a nonprofit that was lobbying to reform the state's beer laws. I got involved. Not long after, I found myself in Montgomery with sweaty ankles, speaking to a House of Representatives subcommittee about why Alabamians should be able to drink the same stuff as people in other states."

Alabama has not historically been known as a hotbed of state-sanctioned libertinism. After the Twenty-First Amendment repealed Prohibition, the state's leaders seized upon section 2 of the amendment, which subjected alcohol to state and local regulations. By limiting the strength of beer to 6 percent and the size of beer containers to less than sixteen ounces, the good people of Alabama would be protected from the evils of intoxication. Further distribution strictures were visited upon would-be brewpub owners, essentially making such businesses economically unfeasible. As a result, beer lovers seeking a craft brew in Alabama in 2004 would have come up with an empty glass.

Enter Free the Hops. When the grassroots advocacy group—made up of architects, doctors, lawyers, and tradesmen with no ties to the beverage industry and no motives beyond the desire to enjoy a good doppelbock or IPA—began visiting the legislature to make their case, they quickly realized that education would be key to their success. One

OPPOSITE:
Good People is
Alabama's
biggest brewery,
and is known for
its hop-forward
ales—including a
double IPA called
Snake Handler.

of the major concerns legislators had was that an increase in ABV would encourage underage drinking. "We had to show the legislators that when teens scrape together enough cash to send someone's older brother to the gas station, they're looking for a major brand and something easy to drink," Stuart continued. "To these kids, an imperial IPA would taste like ashes and cat pee." Stuart also made the economic case for revisiting Alabama's ABV restrictions. "We calculated that the state was losing twenty thousand to thirty thousand dollars a month due to beer runs to other states," he added. "How many jobs might that support? How much tax revenue?"

It took several years, but on Memorial Day weekend in 2009, then-Governor Bob Riley signed legislation allowing an increase from 6 percent to 13.9 percent ABV for beer. "One of our wholesalers took a gamble and stocked his shelves with higher-alcohol beer," Stuart recalled. "That Friday, trucks began going out with Celebrator Doppelbock, Old Rasputin Imperial Stout. Suddenly I didn't have to drive to Georgia to buy stronger beer!"

There were a few more hurdles to jump before Alabama's brewing scene could really soar. In 2011, the Brewery Modernization Act passed, allowing breweries to have an attached taproom. And in 2012, a new container-size law passed, making it possible to sell beer in containers up to 25.9 ounces. With these new laws in place, the number of breweries in Alabama ballooned from two in 2011 to twenty-seven (as of this writing). And Birmingham has four. Stuart offered a rundown of his favorite offerings in his adopted hometown.

"If you visit Birmingham to sample our beer, you have to visit Good People. It was founded in 2008 and is Alabama's biggest brewery, brewing about fifteen thousand barrels a year. Their product is hop-centric—even their brown ale. Good People's IPA has been highly rated in national tastings; their pale and brown ales are the brewer's 'keep the lights on' standbys. They have a double IPA called Snake Handler that gets a lot of attention; I've had people from western states ask me to send them some. People love it, though I can't drink it! Good People does some smaller batch beers too, including a double imperial stout called El Gordo that's 13.9 percent ABV. It's pretty close to perfect, with a consistency between molasses and used engine oil. The artwork they use on their cans reflects the rusty, iron nature of Birmingham's industrial heritage. And the taproom is right across the street from Regions Field, which is the home of the Birmingham Barons minor league baseball team. If the Barons are playing, the atmosphere is especially lively."

Avondale Brewing Company is another must-stop. "Avondale is a four-thousand-barrel brewery that's become the anchor of a regenerated business district. The brewery has punched so far above its weight in terms of economic impact, turning a whole neighborhood around. (Saw's BBQ and Post Office Pies help round out the culinary offerings.) Avondale is doing a good job pushing into new areas, including a souring program. A rather malty saison is their flagship beer; a lot of their beers are Belgian-influenced. They're referred to as 'Hambics'—we're in Birmingham, after all. They're working toward a program where they're souring beers for years. The sour beers appeal to wine drinkers and beer nerds. You're hitting flavors that your brain says are wrong."

Birmingham's current brewery offering is rounded out by Cahaba and Trim Tab. If want to get a broad sense of what's brewing in Alabama, visit the Magic City Brewfest in June.

"There are still neo-Prohibitionists afoot in Alabama," Stuart ventured, "and many have affiliations with conservative religious groups. I'm a born again Christian and was director of a pro-alcohol reform group and see no conflict in this. After all—my Lord's first miracle was not turning water into Kool-Aid."

STUART CARTER is a native of Scotland and a past president of Free the Hops (2007–10).

If You Go

▶ **Getting There:** Birmingham is served by a number of carriers, including Delta (800-221-1212; www.delta.com) and United (800-864-8331; www.united.com).

▶ **Best Time to Visit:** The Magic City Brewfest (www.magiccitybrewfest.com) is generally held in early June. Those sensitive to heat and humidity may wish to avoid the height of summer.

▶ **Spots to Visit:** Good People Brewing Company (205-286-2337; www.goodpeople brewing.com) and Avondale Brewing Company (205-777-5456; www.avondalebrewing.com).

▶ **Accommodations:** A comprehensive list of accommodations is available from the Birmingham Convention & Visitors Bureau (800-458-8085; www.birminghamal.org).

TORDRILLO MOUNTAINS

RECOMMENDED BY **Tommy Moe**

Nothing tops off a great day of skiing like a crisp craft beer. And there are few more inviting places to kick back with a good glass of ale than the Tordrillo Mountains and Tordrillo Mountain Lodge.

The Tordrillos are a compact range seventy-five miles northwest of Anchorage, Alaska's largest city. They rest between the Aleutian Range (to the south) and the Alaska Range (to the west and north) and span some sixty miles north to south. Several peaks eclipse the eleven-thousand-foot mark. A combination of volcanic and glacial activity through the ages has carved an endless array of couloirs and towers; many runs range from three thousand to four thousand vertical feet. (One chute, which the guides have dubbed "Manhattan," is only fifty feet wide and boasts thousand-foot walls!) With an average of six hundred inches of fluffy snow (thanks to its proximity to the Pacific) and some 1.2 million acres of terrain to choose from, fresh powder (or in the spring, soft corn) is always in reach. There's some really extreme terrain available to explore, but there are also immense bowls where skiers or snowboarders of modest ability can experience the thrill of heli-skiing. On clear days—and there are a number of them—you can look out in the distance to see Denali (Mount McKinley), North America's highest peak, at 20,320 feet.

You reach the runs via a Eurocopter A-Star helicopter. A ride in the A-Star sets the tone for a day in the Tordrillos; many visitors are as invigorated by the flight as the skiing. (It's hard to describe the sensation of climbing over—and then falling away from—three-thousand-foot spires.) One of your guides may be Tommy Moe, gold medal winner in the downhill at the 1994 Olympics in Lillehammer, Norway. And your home as you explore the Tordrillos is a five-thousand-square-foot log cabin set on the banks of Judd Lake and the Talachulitna River. The cabin can only be reached by float plane or helicopter, a

OPPOSITE:
The virgin
powder in
Alaska's Tordrillo
Range is nicely
complemented
by ales from
Alaskan Brewing
Company.

roughly forty-five-minute flight from Anchorage. You can look out at two eleven-thousand-foot volcanoes from the deck (as well as Denali) or from the lakeside wood-fired hot tub. During the latter part of the season, it's not uncommon to see black bears and occasionally grizzlies foraging around the lake or exploring surrounding hillsides.

"The hot tub at Tordrillo has to be one of the nicest spots in Alaska to enjoy a beer," Tommy offered. "The days are long, and you can bring a pitcher of beer down from the lodge, slip in the tub, and enjoy. We like to keep nice pale ale on tap at the lodge, some-thing that can appeal to a range of tastes. One of my favorites is the American pale ale from Alaskan Brewing Company. During our spring skiing season, you can stay in the hot tub as late as you want and watch loon—and sometimes moose—come out on the lake. [During Cast and Carve weeks, guests mix spring skiing with salmon and trout fish-ing in the Talachulitna . . . all enabled by the Eurocopter.] The west deck is another great spot to enjoy a beer in the spring and early summer as the sun hangs in the west over the Tordrillos."

Alaska has a population of under 750,000 hearty souls spread over 570,641 square miles, but according to the Brewers Guild of Alaska, the "Last Frontier" supports twenty-seven breweries and brewpubs . . . despite the challenges of transporting equipment and raw materials to such an isolated locale. Anchorage has the greatest concentration of brewpubs, but Alaska's best-known beers hail from the state capital of Juneau in the southeast and Alaskan Brewing Company. The brewery was opened in 1986 by the then-twenty-eighty-year-olds Marcy and Geoff Larson, who had been drawn to Alaska by the state's beauty without a clear vision of exactly how they'd make a living and be able to stay. When pondering what to do to make ends meet, a friend suggested starting a brewery. When Marcy discovered a recipe for a gold rush–era beer that had been originally brewed by the Douglas City Brewing Company (circa 1900) and Geoff brewed a batch, the seeds were sown. That beer would become known as Alaskan Amber and would become the Alaskan Brewing Company's flagship brand.

The summer solstice is a special time to be in the Tordrillos, as the sun never quite sets. It's even more special if you can celebrate it with an evening ski. "It's a tradition at Tordrillo Mountain Lodge that we fly up for a few runs on the solstice after dinner. We'll load up the 'copter around 9:30 and set down above a run—usually something mellow, as everyone has a full stomach. The light is just amazing, a steady alpenglow. We'll make our turns down to the bottom of the bowl, and then break out some snacks—maybe some

Alaskan king crab, crackers, and cheese—and some wine and cans of craft beer. Then we'll toast the solstice, and look around at the great state of Alaska."

TOMMY MOE knew that skiing would be part of his future since his grade school days, when his father let him play hooky to ski powder. What he didn't know was that he would become a World Cup contender and take home the gold in the 1994 Olympics in Lillehammer, Norway—where he won the downhill by .04 of a second—followed by a silver in the super-G. Today, Tommy is a partner and founder of Tordrillo Mountain Lodge. He finds the greatest reward in sharing the property and newly discovered terrain with skiers and snowboarders seeking the trip of a lifetime, whether it's a week of powder skiing in the winter, whitewater rafting the Tal and Coal Creek, or paddleboarding under the summer midnight sun. He resides in Jackson Hole, Wyoming, with his wife, Megan Gerety, and two daughters, Taylor and Taryn.

If You Go

▶ **Getting There:** Guests gather in Anchorage, Alaska, which is served by many carriers. From there, it's a forty-five-minute floatplane ride to Tordrillo Mountain Lodge.

▶ **Best Time to Visit:** Early February through April for ski packages; mid-June through early July for ski/fish packages.

▶ **Spots to Visit:** If you visit Juneau, stop by Alaskan Brewing Company (907-780-5866; www.alaskanbeer.com).

▶ **Accommodations:** Tordrillo Mountain Lodge (907-569-5588; www.tordrillomountain lodge.com) offers a number of all-inclusive ski packages. Captain Cook (907-276-6000; www.captaincook.com) is a popular hotel in Anchorage.

LAKE LOUISE

RECOMMENDED BY **Luis Garcés**

Mountain guide Michael Vincent has called the Fairmont Chateau Lake Louise a four-star resort in a five-star location . . . and this is no slight against the resort! When you walk out of the hotel, you find yourself in the middle of a postcard, with forested hillsides sweeping down to the lake's turquoise waters and Victoria Glacier gleaming in the distance. Chateau Lake Louise offers up vistas that can elevate a good pint to the sublime.

Chateau Lake Louise is set in the midst of Banff National Park, a 2,564-square-mile sanctuary west of Calgary, stretching along much of the southern section of the province of Alberta's border with British Columbia. That the chateau and nearby Banff Springs hotel (another Fairmont property) exist in the national park is thanks in large part to the Canadian Pacific Railway and the laws of supply and demand; the railroad created a supply of westbound train seats, and the hope was that some recreational centers would create a demand. The railway did not underestimate Banff's appeal. Whereas the Banff Springs hotel was built around the hot springs that bubbled up there to appeal to the spa culture, the original structure at Lake Louise—a log chalet with two bedrooms—was built for people interested in mountaineering. In the chalet's early days, several professional Swiss mountain guides were hired and brought to Lake Louise to help guests climb the surrounding mountains. The guides were let go in 1954, but in 1997 the notion of having staff guides was reincarnated. The initial log cabin at Lake Louise burned to the ground, giving way to the monolithic 552-room luxury lodge that sits on what the Stoney Indians called Lake of Little Fishes.

Luis Garcés arrived at Chateau Lake Louise via Mexico's Yucatán Peninsula, with a zeal to introduce guests to the finer points of beer. "When I began working at Fairmont Mayakoba, I was surprised to find that there were no local craft beers featured," he began.

OPPOSITE:
The incredible turquoise waters of Lake Louise are in view from the famed Plain of Six Glaciers trail . . . and several of the bars at Chateau Lake Louise.

"I'm very passionate about beer and wanted to use my knowledge to introduce our guests to some of the fine beers being brewed in Mexico. Working with Cerveceria Calavera, we were able to introduce four craft beers—including an imperial stout—into all the food and beverage outlets at the hotel and train our staff on what makes them different. We also created a light menu pairing food and beer, which was very successful. When I arrived at Chateau Lake Louise, I was curious about the beer offering. The Glacier Saloon, our more casual pub and restaurant, had ten taps and some good beers available. But at the Walliser Stube, our alpine-themed restaurant, there was only Budweiser, Corona, and Kokanee—not the best pairing for the Swiss- and German-inspired cuisine. We explored the notion of instituting beer tastings, but it's not as good a match for this property. People who come to Lake Louise want to be outside to take advantage of the destination."

The focus for many visitors is hiking. One would be hard-pressed to find a richer assortment of day hikes than those originating in the Bow River Valley of southern Banff; overall, the park has six hundred miles of trails. From the chateau, a half mile of walking takes you into wild country; a few hours later, you're back in the comfort of an elegant lodge. The jewel of the extensive trail system around the lake is unquestionably the Plain of Six Glaciers hike. After skirting the lake, the trail climbs abruptly, eventually crossing avalanche paths. Turn a corner soon after, and you walk into an IMAX film. Lake Louise and the chateau are behind you, ahead is the Victoria Glacier, thirty stories tall, and beyond that, Mount Aberdeen, Mount Lefroy, and the Mitre (a mountain shaped like a bishop's hat). Not far ahead, there's the Plain of Six Glaciers Tea House. This structure was initially built as a mountaineering hut by the Swiss guides but now is run seasonally by a local family that serves fresh baked goods and tea. A little farther along, you can take in a vista of all six glaciers: the hanging glaciers on Aberdeen, Lefroy, and Victoria; the Lefroy and Lower Victoria Valley glaciers; and the hanging glacier on Pope's Peak. You'll want to stay alert as you hike along Lake Louise; despite the many sightseers, the region has one of the highest densities of grizzlies in Banff, and bear sightings—usually at a comfortable distance—are not uncommon. (If you're less interested in a hike, consider paddling a canoe across Lake Louise; the reflection of the lodge's red canoes mingling against the white of the glacier in the lake's trademark turquoise waters is mesmerizing.)

Back at the chateau, you can experience those timeless vistas once again, this time with a libation from one of the Fairmont's distinctive pubs. For Luis, the season will dictate the best venue. "If it's summer, I love to sit out on the terrace of the Lakeview Lounge.

The lounge has some good local beers on tap, including Rutting Elk Red, a red ale made by Grizzly Paw Brewing, just down the road in Canmore. Looking out on Victoria Glacier, you can compare notes on the day's hikes with your neighbors and ponder the day you've had in nature. [If you hiked Plain of Six Glaciers and have a pair of binoculars, you can pinpoint exactly where you were earlier in the day.] During cooler weather, it's hard to beat the Walliser Stube, which has a large window looking out on the lake and glacier. Whether you've been out skating on the most beautiful outdoor ice skating rink in the world (Lake Louise), skiing, or dog-sledding (which I'd strongly recommend trying), there's nothing like sitting down with a warm pot of Swiss fondue and a nice glass of Munich Gold from Hacker-Pschorr (Germany) or Stiegl lager (from Austria)."

With Luis's guidance, Fairmont will be adding other distinctive beers to the Walliser Stube's offering soon.

LUIS GARCÉS is Food and Beverage Outlet Manager for the Walliser Stube at Fairmont Chateau Lake Louise in Banff National Park. A native of Veracruz, Mexico, Luis attended Washington State University. During college summers, Luis worked for the San Diego Zoo and San Diego Zoo's Safari Park; after turning twenty-one, he fell in love with the beer that was being brewed in San Diego and throughout the west. Luis joined Fairmont Hotels and Resorts' Leadership Development Program after college and began his career at the Fairmont Mayakoba in the Mexican Mayan Riviera, where he developed a craft beer program.

If You Go

▶ **Getting There:** Alberta is served by many major carriers, including Air Canada (888-247-2262; www.aircanada.com). Lake Louise is roughly one hundred miles to the west.

▶ **Best Time to Visit:** Mid-June through September offers the most reliable weather (and clear trails) for hiking. Winter sports begin mid-November and run into May.

▶ **Spots to Visit:** Glacier Saloon, Lakeview Lounge, and Walliser Stube.

▶ **Accommodations:** The Fairmont Chateau Lake Louise (403-522-3511; www.fairmont.com/lake-louise) has 552 guest rooms.

MELBOURNE

RECOMMENDED BY **Tim Charody**

Say "beer" and "Australia" in the same breath, and the image of a Crocodile Dundee–like character hoisting a huge can of Foster's Lager in proximity to a "barby" might come to mind.

Like so many stereotypes, this one may have had a whiff of truth in earlier times. But those days are gone. Like so many places that were once drowning in uninspired suds, Australia has wholeheartedly embraced the craft beer phenomenon, as Tim Charody explained. "The Australian beer scene is unrecognizable compared to what it was ten years ago (or even five years ago in many places). Before craft beer came along and gave us a few options, in most pubs you could only find one or two different beers to choose from. These were almost always lagers, one being full strength and another mid-strength (and since about ten years ago, a low-carb option popped up as well). If you wanted to drink anything different, you had to go to one of a handful of specialty bars that could be found in the capital cities, and chances are you would struggle to find anyone to go with you, because most people had never even heard of craft beer and sure as hell didn't want to pay more than $4.50 for a beer. The culture was all about quantity not quality. It was about drinking as much of the exact same cheap beer as you possibly could before the bar kicked everyone out onto the street. The main culprit for this beer culture was a law that was introduced after World War I that saw bars and pubs closing their doors and kicking everyone out at six P.M. This led to a phenomenon we called the 'Six O'Clock Swill.' These laws continued up until the late sixties, but the culture remained until quite recently.

"At most pubs these days, you can find at least six to ten beer options (often many more), and the general public is willing to pay a bit more for quality beer (but will generally

OPPOSITE:
Melbourne is on
the cutting edge of
Aussie craft beer.
Cookie Bar is one
of Melbourne's
more eclectic beer
bars and features
fine Thai food.

drink less of them). While Australian beer consumption is at a sixty-five-year low, people are paying more than ever for beer and doing it quite happily."

No city has taken to craft beer like Melbourne. Melbourne may lack a signature opera house, but this vibrant city on Australia's south coast has long been recognized as the nation's cultural capital. Good beer is a perfect complement. "Craft beer is a relatively recent development in the city, and it has gone off like an atomic bomb," Tim enthused. "Melbourne has so much variety and so many little breweries in and around the city. These include KAIJU!, Exit, BrewCult, La Sirène, Cavalier, Kooinda, Moon Dog, Two Birds, Mountain Goat, and Hawthorn. All are considered to be some of the country's finest craft breweries, and they all call Melbourne home. It seems as though every week a new brewery is opening up, and the amount of craft beer–dedicated bars and pubs trumps anywhere else in the country. I wrote a top-ten list for Melbourne back in 2014, and by the time I returned in 2015, I managed to write another top-ten list with an entirely new list of breweries and venues . . . which was whittled down from a list of over thirty! That's how fast this city's beer scene is developing. If you love beer, then you will be busier than a mosquito in a nudist colony in good old Melbourne town."

Walk into almost any pub in Melbourne, and you're likely to find some good craft beer options. Tim shared a few of his favorite beer spots. "Moon Dog is a tiny cult-like brewery hidden in the backstreets of industrial Abbotsford that churns out brews with names like Chocolate Salty Balls, Perverse Sexual Amalgam, and Henry Ford's Girthsome Fjord. While Moon Dog's beers are named with all the attitude of a washed-up rock star, their taste won't let you down either. I guess I love going there because it is exactly what the Melbourne craft beer scene is all about. It's grungy, unpretentious, experimental, and most of all, heaps of fun. If you want to take your taste buds for a ride to the moon and back, then this is the right place. Cookie and Rooftop is another stop. While the elevator ride to the top floor is an adrenaline experience of its own, the ride is definitely worth it. When you do pop out on the rooftop bar above Cookie, you will feel like you have stumbled across Tarzan's bachelor pad nestled high in the trees of the concrete jungle—complete with Astroturf, burger shack, movie screen, and deck chairs. Just downstairs, on level one, is Cookie, with its two hundred–plus beer list from around the planet, a huge line of beer taps, and mouthwatering Thai food to keep you soldiering on. You really can spend all afternoon and night in the same building. Finally, there's the Nest, headquarters of a great Melbourne craft brewery called Two Birds (run by two best friends, Jayne

Lewis and Danielle Allen). While the beers taste amazing fresh out of the brewery, I especially love this place because of the entire bar-dining experience. The restaurant-bar area is located smack-bang in the middle of a working brewery; you can literally smell the beer on the boil and hear the brewers chatting just meters away. There is nothing like sitting back with a fresh pint, watching the brewers buzz around you on forklifts, up and down the sides of fermenting tanks, milling grain and weighing hops."

A few must-tastes from Melbourne's ever-evolving offering include Acid Freaks ("a balsamic vinegar–infused porter brewed by the incredibly adventurous BrewCult"); Mountain Goat's Fancy Pants ("an amber ale that is a perfect balance between sweet toffee malts and light, fruity, spicy hops"); and La Sirène's Praline ("a Belgian praline beer that is literally liquid chocolate, the most incredibly moreish stout you could ever dream of").

TIM CHARODY is one of Australia's premier travel and television presenters, appearing on networks such as ABC, National Geographic, Travel Channel, and Fox Traveller. These days known as the Beer Pilgrim, Tim is out to uncover beer's amazing story. He's hopping around the world, one brew at a time, meeting great characters and digging up fascinating stories, to show there's more to beer than you think.

If You Go

▶ **Getting There:** Melbourne is served by many major carriers from Los Angeles, including Quantas (800-227-4500; www.quantas.com).

▶ **Best Time to Visit:** Melbourne enjoys a temperate climate, with warm to hot summers, mild springs and autumns, and cool winters. The Great Australasian Beer SpecTAPular (www.gabsfestival.com) is generally held in late May.

▶ **Spots to Visit:** Mountain Goat Beer (+61 3 9428 1180; www.goatbeer.com.au); Moon Dog Craft Brewery (+61 3 9428 2307; www.moondogbrewing.com.au); Cookie and Rooftop (+61 3 9663 7660; www.cookie.net.au); The Nest/Two Birds Brewing (+61 03 9762 0000; www.twobirdsbrewing.com.au).

▶ **Accommodations:** Visit Melbourne (www.visitmelbourne.com) lists many lodging options around Melbourne.

| BLANCH WITT | .4L €5,2 | .3L €3,3 |

ANCHOR STEAM .4L €5,7 .3L €4,4
WEIH STEP _ER .5L €4,7 .3L €2,9
SCHREM_ _ZW .5L €4,5 .3L €2,7
TINY REB _PA .4L €7,0 .25 €4,4
TINY REB .4L €6,5 .25L €_
ASPALL CIDER .5L €5,5 .25L €_

TINY RE_ CIDER .4_ €_
TOM OS CIDER .4L €6,5 .25L €4_
BEAVER DOGFISH .4L €7,2 .3L €5,_
ROGUE AMBER .4L €7,2 .3L €5,_

_MAKERS BEER BOARD _

.5L €3,9	.3L €2,7
.5L €4,3	.3L €2,9
.4L €6,8	.3L €5,1
.4L €5,5	.3L €4,2
.4L €6,0	.3L €4,5
.4L €7,3	.3L €5,5
.4L €6,8	.3L €5,1
.4L €6,7	.3L €5,1
€6,0	.3L €4,5

THORNBRIDGE	RED ALE	5,9%	.4L €6,9	.3L €4,9
BRAUWERK	PORTER	5%	.4L €6,8	.3L €5,1
SCHREM SER	DOPPEL MALZ	4,8%	.5L €4,5	.3L €2,7
BEAVER TOWN SM POR_ER		6%	.4L €6_	.3L €5,_
O'HARAS	IRISH STOUT	4,3_	.4_ €5,_	.2_ €_
ROGUE CHOCOLATE _TOUT				€_
LEFFE BRUIN	DUNK_	_%		
MIK KELLER	HOPPY _ILS			
BRAU_				

VIENNA

RECOMMENDED BY **Martin Simion**

The soaring towers of St. Stephen's Cathedral. The lilting voices of the Boys' Choir wafting out from Hofburg Chapel. The uncanny choreography of the Lipizzaner Stallions. The splendor of Schönbrunn Palace.

And a surprising array of beer styles you might not expect from this storied city on the shores of the Danube.

"Most beer lovers know that Vienna is the birthplace of modern lager brewing," Martin Simion began, "and they know of the city's famous wine taverns, or Heurige. But they may not know that, since the early 1990s, many small breweries and brewpubs have sprung up and now are an important part of the city's social scene. Austria has always had an interesting beer scene, but now things are really moving. Vienna once had a number of larger industrial breweries, but today only Ottakringer survives. But even the owners at Ottakringer recognize that the scene is evolving, and now the brewery operates a smaller scale facility to try to introduce patrons to new ideas."

Johann Strauss was wandering the cobblestoned streets of Vienna, likely humming an early version of a coming composition, while Anton Dreher was busy perfecting the process that would lead to lagers as we know them today. Dreher had been born into a brewing family. On a research trip to the United Kingdom in the early 1830s, he was exposed to British malting techniques, which allowed the creation of paler malts. He was taken with the idea of combining lighter malts with bottom-fermented brewing techniques. His early efforts were not completely successful, but in 1841, he came upon the one ingredient that had been lacking—cooler fermenting conditions. He built deep cellars and brought in ice to maintain cooler temperatures during the fermenting—or "lagering"—process. Lager-style beers had appeared erratically around Germany and

OPPOSITE:
As Austria
embraces the craft
beer revolution,
one is as likely
to encounter
American-style
pale ales and
IPAs as Vienna-
style lagers
in bars like
Brickmakers.

Austria at the time, but Dreher's innovation was to standardize the process. The Vienna lager produced was reddish in tint, with a hint of malty sweetness and minimal hop presence, not unlike some Märzens. Thanks to the other breweries Dreher and his family owned, Vienna-style lagers soon spread across Europe. By the end of the century, their popularity had been eclipsed by pale lagers. Vienna-style lagers are not encountered with regularity around Europe today, though they have seen growing acceptance among American beer drinkers.

And beers from abroad are making their way to Vienna. "Many brewers are experimenting with British, American, and Belgian beer styles," Martin continued. "Austrian Märzen—which more resembles a Bavarian helles than a German Märzen—is still the most popular beer in Vienna, but we're also seeing American-inspired pale ales and IPAs, as well as historic German beer styles (like gose or Berliner weisse). Sours are a relatively new category but are also gaining popularity. I just introduced a Flanders red–style beer, and I've been surprised at the positive response. Techniques like dry hopping and barrel aging are being practiced."

Martin shared a few spots he would include on a beer tour of modern Vienna. "After a tour of the historic Ottakringer Brewery [established in 1837], I might stop at the Känguruh Pub. They have a great selection of Belgian beer styles and a very knowledgeable staff. Siebensternbräu would be another place to visit. It's more of a traditional brewpub, with a nice beer garden in the back and traditional Austrian cuisine. [One of the favorites for regular patrons is the hanfbier (hemp beer).] Yppenplatz 4 features the Brauwerk beers from Ottakringer's artisanal efforts. We only do seven barrels per batch, and each beer showcases one of the three main ingredients of brewing. The Belgian blonde is made with sour yeast; a session IPA highlights hops; and a traditional British porter features malt. Yppenplatz also has house-made sausages. The Brickmakers is a tap house that features over thirty carefully selected international beers and pulled pork, spare ribs, and sausages. If you're visiting in summer, you must visit Schweizerhaus. It's famous for its beer garden, which features Budweiser Budvar [from the Czech Republic, not St. Louis] on tap and hearty stelzen. Summer visitors will also want to enjoy a stroll at Donaukanal [a canal that connects to the Danube and flows through the center of town]. The flowing water keeps things nice and cool, and there are countless culinary offerings to enjoy. In December, visitors will enjoy a visit to one of Vienna's many Christkindlmarkts [Christmas markets] to enjoy gluhwein [mulled wine], beer, and food."

Though he makes his living as a brewer, Martin encourages visitors to take in a bit of Vienna's wine culture as well. Vineyards still operate on the city's outskirts, and one has not truly experienced the City of Music until they've sipped a Grüner Veltliner in one of the Heurige. "The classic wine tavern is really an outside sitting area that's connected to a vineyard," he explained. "Only the vineyard's own wine is served." But you shouldn't let the wine tavern owners diminish the significance of beer in Austrian culture. "When the Austrian Independence Treaty was signed in 1955," Martin said, "both wine and beer were served!"

MARTIN SIMION is head brewer at the Ottakringer artisanal brewery in Vienna. Before joining Ottakringer, he was a brewer at Vienna's 1516—one of the city's early brewpubs—and head brewer at Fanø Bryghus in Denmark. Martin is a graduate of Weihenstephan, a branch of the University of Technology Munich, one of the world's leading brewing schools.

If You Go

▶ **Getting There:** Vienna is served by most major carriers.

▶ **Best Time to Visit:** Vienna's inside beer venues are thriving year-round, though the warmer months will allow you to stroll the Donaukanal and other outdoor venues.

▶ **Spots to Visit:** The Ottakringer Brewery (+43 0 1 49 1000; www.ottakringerbrauerei. at); Känguruh Pub (+43 1 597 38 24; www.kaenguruh-pub.at); Siebensternbräu (+43 1 523 86 97; www.7stern.at); Yppenplatz 4 (+43 1 4026644; www.yppenplatz4.at); the Brickmakers (+43 019974414; www.brickmakers.at); Schweizerhaus (+43 1 7280152 0; www.schweizerhaus.at).

▶ **Accommodations:** The Vienna Tourist Board (www.vienna.info) lists a variety of lodging options around the city.

FLANDERS

RECOMMENDED BY **Yannick de Cocquéau**

Prick a Belgian with a pin, and you just might find that lambic, not blood, runs from their veins.

"Everyone in Belgium has beer in their heart and their life," Yannick de Cocquéau observed. "You find beer everywhere, in every situation and every relationship. We have a great concentration of breweries and bars. One feels surrounded by beer! There are a wide range of places to enjoy a beer. Depending on your mood, you can find some place that suits you. Overall, Belgians are drinking less beer than they once did—one hundred years ago, per capita consumption was fifty gallons or more a year! [Now it's dropped to a modest twenty gallons per year.] Today, many people are switching from lager to more specialized beers. There's not much binge drinking. It's about quality and tasting something different, not about quantity."

For such a small country, Belgium cuts a large swath across the universe of beer. Tucked between France, the Netherlands, Germany, and Luxembourg, Belgium is roughly the size of Maryland, but is one of the world's largest exporters of beer . . . and according to the *Economist* magazine, it produces more than 1,100 distinct brands! (If wine is the libation associated with France, beer is most certainly Belgium's beverage.) Belgium is divided along linguistic and political lines. Flanders, in the north, is primarily the domain of the Flemish people, Dutch-speaking Belgians. In Wallonia to the south, French is the primary language. Being along the physical (and philosophical) border between the Germanic and Latin cultures, Belgium has frequently found its soil the site of armed conflicts staged by its larger neighbors, including World Wars I and II. Belgian people are respected for their fortitude and good nature—perhaps a result of enduring so many historical hardships—and their happy-go-lucky attitude may explain their willingness to

OPPOSITE:
The famed
"Barrel
Cathedral" at
Rodenbach—
294 oak casks
bearing
maturating
Flanders red.

appreciate a pint . . . or fluted stem glass. Geography also helped shape the Belgian palate for a wide variety of beer styles and the use of a diversity of brewing ingredients. While the Bavarian beer-purity law *Reinheitsgebot* (which forbids the use of any ingredients beyond water, barley, and hops in brewing) ruled Germany in the north, the French to the south used a variety of ingredients, ranging from herbs and spices to cherries and raspberries. Belgium borrowed from each tradition.

Belgium has a long—very long—brewing history. Barley has been grown in the region's cool climate since at least the third century AD—well before Belgium was Belgium—and the barley was used to brew beer, which proved to be an effective medium for storing the nourishment the grains held. Some of the breweries still operating today date back to the Middle Ages, including one of Belgium's best-known (if less adventurous) brands, Stella Artois. When many outsiders think of brewing and Belgium, monasteries come to mind. In earlier times, monks brewed beer to sell to help cover their costs of operation and to serve to lodgers. Today, there are six true Trappist abbeys left that brew—Orval, Westvleteren, Rochefort, Westmalle, Achel, and the best-known brewing monastery in America, Chimay. According to the International Trappist Association, to be Trappist ale, beer must meet three criteria: 1) The beer must be brewed within the walls of a Trappist abbey or in the direct surroundings, by or under control of Trappist monks; 2) the brewery, the choices of brewing, and the commercial orientations must depend on the monastic community; 3) the economic purpose of the brewery must be directed toward maintenance of the community, assistance and not toward financial profit.

If there are two beer styles that speak to Flanders and the Flemish people, it would be Flanders red ale and lambics. Flanders red—sometimes known as Flanders red-brown—is one of the original "sour ales" and is closely associated with West Flanders. Both sour and sweet to the taste, Flemish reds are generally the result of a mixed fermentation and a blend of younger beer and beer that's been matured up to two years. "It's a beer that's perfect for wine lovers," Yannick continued. "It's the perfect beer to help wine aficionados begin to cross over to beer." The standard bearer of the style is Rodenbach, established in the 1820s in the port town Roeselare by the four brothers Rodenbach. Tours of the Rodenbach facility are available and a must for lovers of Flanders red. "Near the entrance, you pass through the Barrel Cathedral—two hundred and ninety-four perfectly maintained oak casks (*foeders* in Flemish) containing thousands of liters of maturating ale. It's something to walk between the giants."

Lambics are the oldest beer style in the western world, and for some palates, perhaps the oddest. (Gueuze and kriek lambic are derivations of the style, the former a blend of young and matured lambics, the latter fermented with sour cherries.) Yeast, an element in any brewing process, plays an extremely important role in the production of lambics. "Wild" or "spontaneous" yeasts are allowed to descend into open vessels in the breweries, and fermentation continues for several years in wooden casks. "Making lambics requires a brewer with tremendous expertise with yeast," Yannick opined. "It also takes capital, as the beer has to age for a long time." Cantillon Brewery in Brussels is a good place to learn about lambics, or you can stop at the visitor center de Lambiek in Beersel.

No beer pilgrimage to Flanders would be complete without glimpsing at least one Trappist brewery. A trip to Saint Sixtus Westvleteren showcases the hop fields of Poperinge (where 80 percent of Belgian hops are grown) and allows a peek at the most reclusive of Belgium's monastic brewers. Westvleteren's three products—blond, 8 and 12—may only be purchased at the abbey by reservation and from the café In de Vrede across the street (when available). Most agree it's worth the extra effort; Westvleteren's offerings have been recognized on several occasions as the best beer in the world. (Note: You can't visit the monastery itself beyond arranged beer purchases.)

Given the Flemish people's love of beer, it's no surprise that Flanders is awash in beer festivals. "There's at least one festival every weekend, all year long," Yannick described. "There are also many culinary festivals where beer has an important role. More and more restaurants are pairing refined beers with Flemish dishes." Christmas is a special time of year to be in Flanders, and Christmas or winter beers are very popular. "The tradition dates back to the time before refrigeration, and brewers had to empty their storage spaces to make room for new hops and malts in the early fall. As everything had to go, brewers were given more leeway to make what they wanted—it was a chance for brewers to show regular clients what they really could do. The beers were usually ready by the end of the year, and they tended to be more alcoholic and use lots of spices. It was part of their experimental nature.

"Nowadays, brewers could make these kinds of beers all year long. But they keep it as an end-of-year tradition."

YANNICK DE COCQUÉAU is Product Manager for Flanders for Foodies at VISITFLANDERS, in charge of everything concerning beer and tourism in Flanders and Brussels. Beside this "professional activity" he's active in the local beer consumers association, Zythos, and its annual Zythos Bier Festival. As a beer sommelier, Yannick also gives lectures with beer as a central theme. He also likes to brew at home.

If You Go

▶ **Getting There:** You'll want to fly to Brussels, which is served by many international carriers. The beer regions to the west are a short drive away.

▶ **Best Time to Visit:** The Flanders beer culture is thriving year-round, though mid-April to mid-October sees the nicest weather. The Christmas season showcases many holiday beers.

▶ **Spots to Visit:** Rodenbach Brewery (+32 0 51 27 27 00; palmbreweries.com); Cantillon Brewery (+32 2 521 49 28; www.cantillon.be); Saint Sixtus Westvleteren (+32 0 57 40 03 76; www.sintsixtus.be); In de Vrede (+32 0 57 40 03 77; www.indevrede.be).

▶ **Accommodations:** Visit Flanders (212-584-2336; www.visitflanders.com) details lodging options in the Flemish region of Belgium and provides an excellent beer overview.

PUNTA GORDA

RECOMMENDED BY **Todd Calitri**

Belize (formerly known as British Honduras) is tucked between the Mexican state of Quintana Roo to the north, Guatemala and Honduras to the west and south, and the Caribbean to the east. Many visitors are drawn to the small nation's coastal regions and the attractions of the Mesoamerican Barrier Reef, which stretches along the entire Belizean coast and is the second-largest barrier reef in the world. Others are drawn to the interior, where much of the original rain forest is intact.

Visitors to the southern Belize village of Punta Gorda needn't choose, as here the jungle stretches to the sea—and the adjacent Gulf of Honduras offers one of the world's most celebrated saltwater fisheries.

"I first came to Belize in the mid-1990s, to Ambergris Caye, which is in the north," Todd Calitri began. "A few years later I was there with my employer, who owns a number of interests around Belize. Some conservationists were soliciting him for donations on Ambergris. Seeing all the development already underway on the island, he said, 'Show me a place that's still intact.' They immediately flew south to Punta Gorda. It was the old Belize, undeveloped, where the rainforest meets the ocean. Not long after, my employer purchased a fishing lodge a bit inland, now known as Belcampo."

Belcampo sits on a hilltop five miles inland from the Caribbean and includes a main lodge and sixteen suites set along the hillside in the midst of the rainforest. Several hundred acres of land below the lodge are given over to Belcampo's organic farm, where fifty varieties of fruit and vegetables are grown and pigs, chickens, and lambs are raised. (More than 80 percent of the food that's served at Belcampo is harvested from the farm, and it's served fresh.) Seven thousand cacao plants have been planted on the hillsides surrounding the farm, the foundation of what will soon be an artisan-chocolate operation.

Sugar cane is also being raised—raw material for a rum distillery on the property.

The farm and its bounties are central to the Belcampo experience. Guests can partake in a number of tours of the property's various gardens, go foraging in the forest with a local guide, and participate in cooking demonstrations. One tour, "Snorkel with the Chef," takes guests to the Gulf of Honduras, where Chef Renee Driscoll and her crew dive for conch, lobsters, and lionfish. (Your catch is grilled up on the boat.) Another favorite agritourism activity is Belcampo's Bean to Bar Chocolate Class. After a tour of the organic gardens, the genesis of chocolate is explained. There's a hand-on demonstration of how plants are grafted, and how cacao pods—which resemble a large squash—are cut to release the seeds, the source of chocolate. There's even a chance to partake in the blending process. Guests take away fresh chocolate bars with 70 percent cacao.

The fish that attract anglers to Punta Gorda, permit, are considered the holy grail for Caribbean light-tackle anglers. Permits' aerodynamics give them tremendous strength; specimens, which can run from five to forty pounds, have been known to rip 150 yards of line out in their first run. Permit are renowned as the spookiest creatures of the flats; to catch one on a fly, you have to do many things right—cast a heavy fly forty or fifty feet, often into whipping winds, mimic the halting gait of a crab with your retrieve, and play a very strong fish on light line. The Garbutt Brothers—Scully, Oliver, and Eworth—and their team have gained a stellar reputation for leading anglers to permit. Permit fishing is a team sport; your guide pushes the boat along with a long pole while scanning the shallows from a platform. When he spots a fish, it's the angler's job to land their fly gently in front of the fish . . . and hope it's interested. Anglers can go many days (or even years!) without landing a permit. But when you do, a cold beer is in order.

In Punta Gorda, that beer will almost certainly be a Belikin. Belikin (made by the Belize Brewing Company) does not have a monopoly in Belize, though you'll have to work hard to find something different. Belize is not IPA country; given the heat, a crisp Belikin lager is a good match for post-fishing activities. If you're seeking something a bit more spirited, Belikin Brewing Company also brews a stout. A seasonal brew—the Chocolate Stout—includes nibs of cacao and is a perfect after-dinner treat. (You'll find that Belikins go down particularly easy. It's not just the pleasure of a cold beer in a hot climate; Belikin bottles hold only 9.6 ounces!)

"When I've had a good day on the water—and they're all good, whether you land a permit or not—there are two great places to celebrate," Todd shared. "The first is the top

OPPOSITE:
Sipping a Belikin on the top deck at Belcampo, you can enjoy views of the Rio Grande, the Belize rainforest, and the Caribbean.

deck at Belcampo. The Caribbean is there in the distance. The fruit trees in the foreground attract a variety of bird life, including toucans. More often than not, there's a chorus of howler monkeys accompanying you as you recount the day's adventures. The other is at the bar at Garbutt's. You can grab your Belikin, walk out onto the side deck above Joe Taylor Creek, and hoot at the other guides as they come in with their fishermen. Local people driving by wave. You feel like you're at the center of life in Punta Gorda."

TODD CALITRI ("T. C.") comes from a long line of educators and fly fishermen. Before coming to Belcampo, T. C. ran the Alaska Sportsman's Lodge for fourteen years. He has also worked for the Nature Conservancy on Palmyra Atoll as a boat captain and head guide. Todd has guided trout in Colorado, worked as a guide in the Florida Keys and West Coast, and worked as a fly-shop employee. He has also worked extensively with Orvis travel and has hosted a number of international saltwater seminars in both Belize and the Bahamas. You can contact him directly at tc@belcampobz.com should you have any questions about fly fishing in Southern Belize.

If You Go

▶ **Getting There:** A number of carriers provide service to Belize City, including United (800-864-8331; www.united.com) and Delta (800-221-1212; www.delta.com). Tropic Air (800-422-3435; www.tropicair.com) provides service from Belize City to Punta Gorda.

▶ **Best Time to Visit:** November through May is the high season.

▶ **Spots to Visit:** Belcampo (888-299-9940; www.belcampobz.com) is open for overnight guests as well as lunch and dinner visitors. Anglers—whether they've caught a permit or not—will want to hoist at least one Belikin at Garbutt's Fishing Lodge (501-722-0070; www.garbuttsfishinglodge.com).

▶ **Accommodations:** If Belcampo and Garbutt's are full, the Punta Gorda website (www.puntagordabelize.com) lists other lodging options.

VANCOUVER ISLAND

RECOMMENDED BY **Joe Wiebe**

Vancouver Island stretches almost three hundred miles north to south, at times separated from the mainland by only a few miles. The island is considered one of the world's most diverse ecosystems, combining rainforests, mountain ranges, and more than two thousand miles of coastline. Its natural beauty, abundant outdoor activities (kayaking, fishing, surfing, golf . . . and on and on), a thriving art scene, and British charm (overhear some residents of Victoria chatting and you'd swear you were in London) have helped it become one of the most beloved islands in the world.

These days, you can add a vibrant brewing culture to the mix of Vancouver Island's attractions.

"When I first moved out to Victoria from Ontario in the 1990s, there was a lot of talk of a bridge connecting the island to the mainland," Joe Wiebe recalled. "I remember the arguments on the island against the project. People weren't concerned about the cost. They didn't want to be connected to the mainland. Many people feel they are separate from the rest of British Columbia and like it that way. Islanders value their independence and self-sufficiency. There's a strong ethic of supporting island businesses. I think this attitude has done a lot to foster Vancouver Island's craft beer scene. Residents support island breweries; they don't care too much about beer from other places."

For all intents and purposes, Canada's craft beer revolution began on Vancouver Island in 1984, with the opening of Spinnakers Brewpub in Victoria, British Columbia's provincial capital, which is located at the southern end of the island. "There was a short-lived microbrewery that opened in 1982 in Horseshoe Bay, north of Vancouver," Joe explained, "but it didn't last long. Spinnakers was the first brewpub in Canada and among the first in North America. Paul Hadfield was the building's architect, and after a few

years became the proprietor. Spinnakers was ahead of its time. When the first big craft brewer's convention was held down in Portland, they commissioned a bus to take attendees up to Spinnakers, as it was a model that didn't exist elsewhere. In the early nineties, Spinnakers adopted a slow-food movement approach, working with local farmers to source ingredients. They have a beautiful spot on the inner harbor, a great kitchen, and a great assortment of beer." Spinnakers was joined later in 1984 by Vancouver Island Brewing, and every few years thereafter, a new brewery or brewpub opened. Now greater Victoria boasts twelve such establishments, covering a gamut of styles and approaches and earning the city the unofficial moniker of Canada's craft beer capital.

A ramble along Victoria's Beer Mile will provide visitors with a great sense of what the city has to offer. "There's a ring of four brewpubs around the upper harbor, and there are five more brewpubs close by," Joe continued. "It's only a fifteen-minute walk from the heart of downtown. When Spinnakers was built, it was an unused area. The city didn't really know what to do with a brewpub and sent Paul and his partners over there. Now there's a walkway, hotels, condos. A few favorites (in addition to Spinnakers) include Canoe Brewpub, beside Victoria's iconic Blue Bridge. Built in 1894, the brewpub was originally the City Lights Building, Victoria's electricity plant. Canoe was restored in 1996 with dramatic vaulted ceilings and the city's best westward-facing deck. I would also visit Swans, which is just a few doors down. It was originally a feed warehouse and was beautifully renovated, and includes an art collection. A little off the Beer Mile, but very worth a visit, is Driftwood Brewing. Driftwood is one of British Columbia's best breweries. Their Fat Tug IPA has become the flagship beer of BC craft brewing. It stands up to the best IPAs coming out of Portland, though it's very hard to find outside of the province, as Driftwood can't keep up with demand here. It's the beer that beer writers drink when they visit Victoria."

Greater Victoria is not the only hotbed of Vancouver Island brewing. The mid-island is also seeing a beer renaissance. On the east side of the island, it's in Courtenay/Comox and Cumberland, on the west, Tofino. "The Cumberland region has historically relied on coal mining," Joe said. "Cumberland and Courtenay were Lucky towns—that is, places where residents consumed a lot of Lucky Lager, a brand owned by Labatt that was produced on Vancouver Island. Now there's a new scene developing. A lot of young families are moving in—in Cumberland, it seems that everywhere you look there are couples with strollers and a growler hanging off the handle. Then you have Cumberland Brewing,

OPPOSITE:
Victoria—
Canada's
unofficial craft
beer capital—
boasts four
brewpubs along
its picturesque
upper harbor.

DESTINATION 8

which is in an old pizza restaurant. The pizza maker used to be a brewer and was eventually convinced to get back into the brewing game. In Courtenay, there's Gladstone Brewing, which operates in an old garage. Forbidden is also there, a nanobrewery based in the Westerly Hotel.

"The first mid-island brewery was over in Tofino, on the west coast. Tofino is a beautiful spot, celebrated for its surfing and kayaking. Any visitor to Vancouver Island should try to fit it into their itinerary. Tofino Brewing was started by some guys who'd moved to the area for its natural amenities but missed craft beer. They started off thinking they'd follow the traditional wholesale model—sell kegs to restaurants, bottle some. But there was a twist, in that they'd also sell growlers. This was partially from an environmental philosophy; they wanted to generate less garbage. They bought three hundred growlers for the week they opened, and they sold out. They ordered six hundred more, and they were gone in another week. Then they ordered a thousand, and those eventually sold. Tofino Brewing's growler sales had eclipsed the town's population [1,800]."

NOTE: If you make your way to Vancouver Island via the city of Vancouver, be sure to check out the city's burgeoning brewing culture. Thanks to changes in laws relating to on-premises sales, many new breweries have opened with accompanying tasting lounges, and existing sites have also opened lounges. "The lounges are fairly small; most have thirty to thirty-five seats," Joe explained. "It's a very neighborhood-focused scene, but there's great energy, with many young people over the moon for new beers." One of the greatest concentrations of breweries (as of this writing) is in the Mount Pleasant neighborhood, where Brassneck, 33 Acres, and Main Street Brewing are within five minutes of each other.

JOE WIEBE is the Thirsty Writer. He writes mainly about craft beer, as well as wine, spirits, sports, and travel, for a wide range of print and online publications. Joe is a co-founder of Victoria Beer Week and the author of *Craft Beer Revolution: An Insider's Guide to BC Breweries* (Douglas & McIntyre, second edition released in 2015). Read more at www.thirstywriter.com.

If You Go

▶ **Getting There:** Visitors will either fly to Victoria, which is served by several carriers, including Air Canada (888-247-2262; www.aircanada.com) and Horizon Air (800-252-7522; www.alaskaair.com); or take the ferry from Washington State or Vancouver. Ferry options are highlighted at www.hellobc.com.

▶ **Best Time to Visit:** Vancouver has a temperate climate, though visitors arriving in late fall and winter can anticipate a good deal of rain.

▶ **Spots to Visit:** Spinnakers Gastro Brewpub (250-386-2739; www.spinnakers.com); Swans Brewpub (800-668-7926; www.swanshotel.com); Canoe Brewpub (250-361-1940; www.canoebrewpub.com); Driftwood Brewery (250-381-2739; www.driftwoodbeer.com); Cumberland Brewing (250-400-2739; www.cumberlandbrewing.com); Gladstone Brewing (250-871-1111; www.gladstonebrewing.ca); Forbidden Brewing (www.forbidden brewing.com); Tofino Brewing (250-725-2899; www.tofinobrewingco.com).

▶ **Accommodations:** Tourism Victoria (800-663-3883; www.tourismvictoria.com) offers a comprehensive list of lodging options in Victoria, Cumberland/Courtenay, and Tofino.

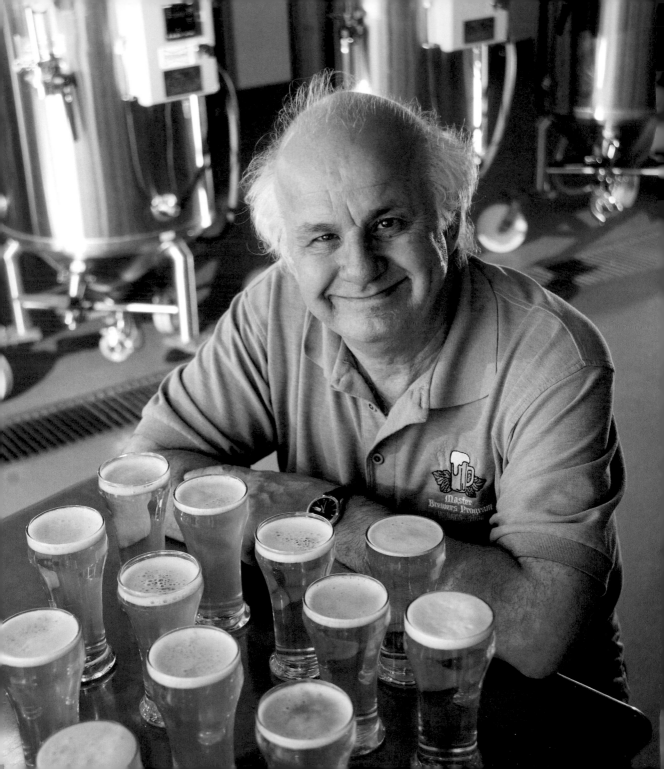

DAVIS

RECOMMENDED BY **Dr. Charles Bamforth**

Rock 'n' roll fantasy camps have sprung up stage left and right in recent years, giving air-guitar avatars and assorted wannabes a chance to rub shoulders under the klieg lights with slightly past-their-prime rock stars. There is an equivalent for homebrewing enthusiasts. But instead of being holed up for the weekend with the bassist from a slightly forgotten eighties hair band, you'll be learning at the feet of a veritable brewing hall of famer—Dr. Charles Bamforth—at the August A. Busch III Brewing and Food Science Laboratory of the University of California, Davis.

"We attract three basic types of people to the Introduction to Practical Brewing Class," Charlie began. "First, there are the homebrewers who want to improve their craft. They're quite passionate—sometimes their beer goes well, sometimes not so well. They really want to understand how and why things happen. The second type of attendee is the homebrewer that's hoping to gain the skill set to make a career out of it—develop their own brewing company. The other group that comes to Davis consists of people who are already in the brewing industry, perhaps working in a smaller company seeking greater knowledge, or with a bigger company but in a nontechnical role."

The University of California, Davis, sits amidst rolling farmland fifteen miles east of the Golden State's capital city, Sacramento. From the early twentieth century, UC Davis has been lauded for its contributions to agricultural science and animal husbandry. With the growth of the wine industry in nearby Napa and Sonoma counties. Davis's beer curricula, which has been part of the university's offering since 1958, gained momentum with the growing popularity of craft beer in the nineties and rocketed to prominence with the recruitment of Charlie Bamforth to lead the program in 1999. Charlie came to California as the Anheuser-Busch Endowed Professor of Malting and Brewing Sciences

OPPOSITE: Dr. Charlie Bamforth—the "Pope of Foam"—shares his thirty-plus years of professional brewing experience with home brewers at UC Davis Extension's introductory brewing courses.

DESTINATION 9

after twenty-one years in Great Britain's brewing industry. Alumnae of Davis's brewing program dot the craft beer landscape.

Charlie explained the genesis of the week-long programs geared toward hobbyists. "Extension programs, even those for master brewers, had previously been very theoretical. When I came to Davis, we were able to build a gleaming brewery complete with four smaller brewhouses. I wanted to see it used. What better way to teach brewing than to grind down the dust of the science in the classroom and then cross the corridor to a hands-on setting in a real brewery. I'm not paid to do the classes, but the money we raise gets ploughed back into my program so I can maintain the facility, employ my brewer, even expand the facilities. The National Institutes of Health isn't likely to send me money to brew beer; the introductory classes help support our work. It's a win-win."

According to an American Homebrewer's Association study conducted in 2013, there are an estimated 1.2 million homebrewers in America. Given this considerable population of enthusiasts, gaining entry to one of the sixty coveted spots in Introduction to Practical Brewing (which is offered four times a year) is a tall order. If you're able to score one of the spots, Charlie described what you can expect.

"In the classroom, we cover everything from raw materials to finished product. Why different barleys have (or don't have) suitable properties for brewing; how to make a great malt; the significance of water and how different chemical properties in the water can influence the end product; how different hops and hop preparations influence flavor, why you use them at various stages of the brewing process, and benefits beyond flavor; and different types of yeast and the role yeast plays. Many discussions surround quality—how to get the right color, the proper clarity, the right head. After all, they call me the Pope of Foam. We also look at the systems necessary to ensure quality for different levels of production—homebrewer or commercial brewer. The atmosphere is very informal and relaxed, with a good deal of banter. For many participants, it's a chance to have an informal conversation with someone who's been there and done that. I often say that the brewing industry is full of opinions. As long as you listen to mine, you'll be fine!

"In the brewery, each student gets to brew in our 1.5-barrel brewery. It's as fancy as any brewery anywhere. Students don't just push knobs; the experience is very hands-on. There's also a chance to brew on one of the smaller systems. To get perspective on the behind-the-scenes operations of a real craft brewery, we visit Sudwerk. The brewmaster there walks us through the operation, including the laboratory and packaging facility.

"We have a tasting at the end of the week, though the beer the students have produced is very young. We also taste some beers that students have brought along. Some of it's good, some less so. One student asked me to taste the beer he'd made. I did and told him that it smelled like halitosis. He asked why, and I responded that he hadn't brought the wort to a vigorous enough boil to drive off any nasty flavors. He called me a few weeks later and said, 'You've cost me a lot of money.' I asked how, and he replied that he'd felt compelled to buy a new brewery."

DR. CHARLES BAMFORTH is distinguished professor and leader of malting and brewing studies at the University of California, Davis. He has more than thirty-seven years of academic and professional brewing expertise, including senior roles with Brewing Research International and Bass Brewers. Charlie's current research program focuses primarily on the wholesomeness of beer, including studies on the psychophysics of beer perception, on polyphenols, and on the residues from non-starchy polysaccharide digestion that constitute soluble fiber and potential prebiotics in beer. He has published many papers on the topic and a number of books, including *Beer Is Proof God Loves Us*. Charlie has received the Award of Distinction from the American Society of Brewing Chemists and the Cambridge Prize from the Institute of Brewing & Distilling. Unbeknownst to many of his beer acolytes, Charlie is also a passionate soccer fan and an accomplished soccer writer. His efforts include countless articles and a book, *In Keeping with the Wolves*.

If You Go

► **Getting There:** Visitors to Davis can fly into Sacramento, which is served by most major domestic carriers.

► **Best Time to Visit:** UC Davis Extension's (800-752-0881; https://extension.ucdavis.edu) introductory brewing courses are offered four times a year.

► **Spots to Visit:** You'll be busy most of the week, but you will pop over to Sudwerk (530-758- 8700; www.sudwerk.com) at least once.

► **Accommodations:** The Yolo County Visitors Bureau (530-297-1900; www.visityolo.com) highlights lodging options in Davis and the vicinity.

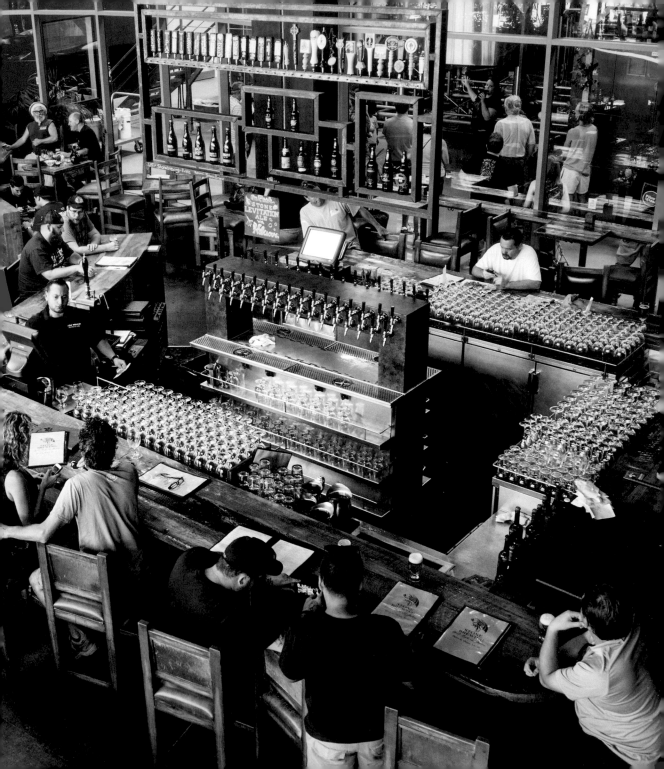

SAN DIEGO

RECOMMENDED BY **Greg Koch**

One quality that many great beer towns share is slightly dreary weather, at least for a portion of the year. Such cooler, wet weather, the thinking goes, drives people inside to places like pubs. People who frequent pubs drink more beer, come to appreciate more interesting styles, and hence provide a ready and eager market for would-be brewers.

San Diego turns this theory on its head. The city enjoys 146 sunny days and 117 partly sunny days, with an average temperature of 70.5 degrees. San Diego's limited water resources are wisely channeled toward brewers, it would seem, as there are some forty breweries in the city limits, as of this writing, and over one hundred in San Diego County.

Greg Koch—CEO and cofounder of Stone Brewing—traces his craft beer epiphany to 1987 and a pint of Anchor Steam beer in Los Angeles, where he was living at the time. "It was the first beer that gave me the idea there could be something beyond the yellow fizzy stuff we see in commercials, and I was intrigued. When I discovered the existence of brewpubs, I went down the rabbit hole. I became a beer enthusiast. Eventually, that led me to take a brewing class at University of California, Davis, and it was there that I ran into Steve Wagner—my partner in crime for Stone Brewing. I was an uber beer geek and Steve was an avid, talented homebrewer. We started talking about our mutual passion and realized we were coming at it from different angles but to a similar point. That was where Stone got going. Steve was also living in Santa Monica at the time, and we began hatching a plan. I think we were the first brewers in San Diego to show you could go your own way and it could be successful. At the time, most brewers were doing tame things. We wanted to break out and do more creative beers, more hop-forward and bigger character."

Considering San Diego's brewing history, the city's rise to prominence as a craft beer hotbed is not surprising. Several notable breweries operated in the city before Prohibition,

OPPOSITE:
Stone Brewing's
Escondido
brewery
and adjacent
World Bistro
& Gardens
are among
San Diego's most
popular tourist
attractions.

DESTINATION 10

including the San Diego Brewing Company, Mission Brewery, and Aztec Brewery, just across the Mexican border in Mexicali. (Aztec was well-positioned to serve thirsty San Diegans once Prohibition arrived, as was Tijuana, which added nearly two hundred cantinas to meet demand.) Once the Twenty-First Amendment was enacted, several brewers returned, providing a substantial portion of the beer brewed in the state of California. But as in so many other markets, the expansion of the national behemoths slowly suppressed local production until the early fifties, when commercial brewing in San Diego ceased. Though commercial efforts may have been squashed under giant Clydesdale hooves, the region harbored a subculture of homebrewers, including clubs like QUAFF (Quality Ale and Fermentation Fraternity) and Foam on the Brain. (By the early nineties, San Diego's homebrewers were greatly abetted by Home Brew Mart, a supply store that eventually spawned Ballast Point Brewing Company.) It took San Diegans a few years to embrace the brewpub trend once California legalized the concept in 1982, but with the opening of Karl Strauss's Old Columbia Brewery and Grill in 1989, the door was edged open. Once Stone came on the scene in 1996, the door was kicked off its hinges.

There are many fine brewers thriving in the bright San Diego sun. Ballast Point, Green Flash, AleSmith, and Port Brewing Company/The Lost Abbey (among others) have all received great acclaim. But no brewer has received more praise than Stone; *BeerAdvocate* magazine has named Stone "All-Time Top Brewery on Planet Earth." Given this, any beer traveler visiting the area should place a stop at Stone high on their itinerary. You won't be alone. "Our Escondido location is the third-most-popular visitor attraction in north San Diego County, behind Legoland and the San Diego Zoo Safari Park," Greg continued. "People come from all over the world to visit their mecca, which is extraordinarily flattering. We give more than fifty-five thousand guests our tour each year. It costs three dollars; after the tour, visitors have a tasting of four Stone beers and receive a keepsake taster glass. One dollar from the tour fee goes to a local charity." Most visitors will linger at the adjacent Stone Brewing World Bistro & Gardens for a bit more tasting (thirty-six beers on tap) and some of the kitchen's organic fare.

Given the size of San Diego County and its brewery abundance, a few strategic visits to local beer bars might be in order to maximize your tasting experience. "One of my favorite places to hang out is Neighborhood [in the East Village neighborhood]. It's a great little gastropub and was one of the early leaders in craft beer bars. [The current list boasts nearly thirty local brews.] There's also Craft & Commerce, another great place in Little

Italy." Toronado, the famed multitap house hailing from San Francisco's Lower Haight Street neighborhood, also has an outpost in the North Park neighborhood.

San Diegans enjoy being outside—who can blame them with that weather—and Greg Koch has envisioned Stone's eclectic farm-to-table restaurants as places where visitors can enjoy both great beer and fresh air. This philosophy extends to the Liberty Station location in the Point Loma neighborhood, once a naval training center. The almost 55,000-square-foot space includes several indoor and outdoor dining areas and bars, a bocce ball court, a movie courtyard, and an immense garden. "We have forty taps at Liberty Station," Greg said, "and a lot of guest taps. I find the outside areas a very relaxing place to have a beer. I usually prefer a classic West Coast IPA, something with 6.5 percent to 7.2 percent ABV. Crisp, refreshing, distinctively bitter, with floral, piney, and citrus overtones.

"Some people argue this style of beer should be called a San Diego pale ale."

GREG KOCH is CEO and co-founder of Stone Brewing, the ninth largest craft brewing company in the United States. An avid craft beer enthusiast and world traveler, Koch can often be found among imbibers across the planet.

If You Go

▶ **Getting There:** San Diego is served by most major carriers.
▶ **Best Time to Visit:** You'll find fine weather in San Diego pretty much all the time . . . though May and June can see some clouds. San Diego Beer Week (https://sdbw.org) is generally held in early November.
▶ **Spots to Visit:** Stone Brewing (760-294-7899; www.stonebrewing.com) in Escondido and Liberty Station; Neighborhood (619-446-0002; www.neighborhoodsd.com); Craft & Commerce (619-269-2202; www.craft-commerce.com); Toronado (619-282-0456; www.toronadosd.com).
▶ **Accommodations:** The San Diego Tourism Authority (619-232-3101; www.sandiego.org) lists a range of lodging options.

SAN FRANCISCO

RECOMMENDED BY **Mark Carpenter**

In the opening paragraph of *McTeague*, Frank Norris's classic novel of late nineteenth-century San Francisco life, the title character stops for some beer after his regular Sunday dinner:

> On his way back to his office, one block above, he stopped at Joe Frenna's saloon and bought a pitcher of steam beer. It was his habit to leave the pitcher there on his way to dinner. . . . By and by, gorged with steam beer, and overcome by the heat of the room, the cheap tobacco, and the effects of his heavy meal, he dropped off to sleep.

Things don't go too well for McTeague as the story unfolds. But he was on to something with his appetite for Steam Beer, a beverage that put San Francisco on the beer map before there even were beer maps.

"I'm amazed at how popular beer has become," Mark Carpenter began. "Now, much of the credit for ingenuity that used to go to winemakers goes to brewers. People have a new appreciation of beer. When I first started brewing, people would say, 'What's Anchor?' I have children in their mid-thirties now, and it's funny to have them tell me that their friends want to meet me."

Jim Koch and his Boston Beer Company may have done more than anyone to bring the idea of craft beer to America through its aggressive advertising campaigns. But a strong case can be made that the first shots of the microbrewery revolution were fired in San Francisco, when Fritz Maytag decided to get into the beer business. "Fritz was a student at Stanford, and he used to come up to San Francisco and have dinner at the Old Spaghetti Factory in the North Beach neighborhood," Mark continued. "He fell in love

OPPOSITE:
Anchor Brewing
Company dates
back to 1896,
and laid the
groundwork
for America's
craft brewing
revolution in
the 1970s under
Fritz Maytag's
guidance.

with the city and Anchor Steam beer. The Old Spaghetti Factory was owned by a Chicagoan named Freddy Kuh. Fritz and Freddy became friends, and Freddy told Fritz he should go visit the brewery. He felt that steam beer was part of San Francisco history. It was failing, and he should see it before it went away. Fritz did go see it. At that time, it was a nineteenth-century brewery—only one pump, no refrigeration. Nonetheless, he ended up buying it. He realized that if he was going to make money, the beer would have to be consistent and would have to be bottled. He started down the path to achieve these goals. At the time, there were under one hundred breweries across the country. The few other small breweries were making regular yellow beer, trying to compete with the national brands. The only way they could survive was by selling it cheaper. Fritz couldn't make money selling beer cheaper; he had to sell it at a higher price. But he had something unique—steam beer. Many thought he couldn't do it, but he decided he would go down trying. It took nine years to start making money, but he had a vision of where he wanted to go and kept at it. And then, in the mid-seventies, the market began to change."

Indeed it did. Anchor Steam came to be recognized as one of America's great beers, a forerunner of the many thousands of flavorful American-brewed beers to come. Anchor Porter, Liberty Ale, Old Foghorn Barleywine Style Ale, and the first annual Christmas Ale followed in 1975. America's first craft brewery was on firm footing.

What is Steam Beer, and how did it get its name? Steam Beer is a hybrid of sorts, a beer fermented with lager yeast at temperatures associated with ales in open-air fermenters, through a process called kräusening. According to Anchor historians, the name stems from a nineteenth-century nickname applied to all beers brewed on the West Coast under primitive conditions and without ice. While the etymology is not completely clear, it likely relates to the original practice of fermenting the beer on San Francisco's rooftops. The foggy night air naturally cooled the fermenting beer in lieu of ice, creating steam off the warm open pans. The Anchor Brewing Company tour showcases the kräusening process, and guests receive generous samples of Anchor product. "I really like how the tour begins with our beautiful old copper brewhouse," Mark added. "It draws you in. I think the sense of handcrafting comes across; there's not just rows of stainless tanks and people in front of computers."

There are approximately fifteen breweries/brewpubs in San Francisco proper, down from the one hundred that operated there at the time of *McTeague*. Cast a net up to Marin, over to the East Bay, and down to Silicon Valley, and that number is multiplied many times. Mark shared a few of his favorites. "If you had a clear day, I'd head out to the Beach Chalet at the western edge of Golden Gate Park overlooking the Pacific. They have good beer and food, but the building's a great attraction. It was built during the Great Depression and features great WPA murals. Over in Haight-Ashbury, right near the old Grateful Dead House, there's Magnolia Brewing. They do fabulous beer; I especially like their Kalifornia Kolsch."

When asked where he likes to enjoy a pint of his own handiwork, Mark didn't hesitate. "I like Tadich Grill down in the financial district. It's San Francisco's oldest restaurant. [Tadich was established in 1849; it's also California's oldest restaurant.] Toronado, in the Lower Haight, is another great spot. It's one of the original great beer bars and introduced people to many interesting beers. [It's also one of the few places where one can frequently find Pliny the Elder, Russian River Brewing Company's much lauded double IPA, on tap.] And though the Old Spaghetti Factory is long gone, there are lots of bars in North Beach—Tosca, Specs, and Vesuvio, across Jack Kerouac Alley from City Lights Books."

MARK CARPENTER is head brewer at Anchor Brewing Company.

If You Go

▶ **Getting There:** San Francisco is served by most major carriers.

▶ **Best Time to Visit:** San Francisco has a Mediterranean climate. You can count on some rain in the winter, some fog in the summer (especially in the city's western reaches), and generally beautiful, sunny falls.

▶ **Spots to Visit:** Anchor Brewing Company (415-863-8350; www.anchorbrewing.com); Beach Chalet (415-386-8439; www.beachchalet.com); Magnolia Pub (415-864-7468; www.magnoliapub.com); Tadich Grill (415-391-1849; www.tadichgrill.com); Toronado (415-863-2276; www.toronado.com); Tosca (415-986-9651; www.toscascafesf.com); Specs (415-421-4112); Vesuvio (www.vesuvio.com). Reservations are necessary for the Anchor Brewing tour.

▶ **Accommodations:** A good place to start your planning is the San Francisco Convention and Visitors Bureau (415-391-2000; www.sfvisitor.org).

DESTINATION 11

HONG KONG

RECOMMENDED BY **Toby Cooper**

The Special Administrative Region of Hong Kong rests on the southeastern coast of China. Its strategic location has made it an important trading center for countless generations. Hong Kong was maintained as a British colony until 1997, when it was handed back to China. Many reminders of Great Britain's 150-plus years of influence remain, ranging from architecture to streets named for British personages to the sound of English in sidewalk conversations. One facet of English culture that was missing in Hong Kong was good beer. But publican Toby Cooper has been working to right that affront since 2003.

"I've been in Hong Kong since 1996," he began. "For a number of years, the only good beer available was a few British and Belgian imports. As far as local people were concerned, beer was a working-class thirst quencher, a cheap drink that goes with a simple dinner. A few small breweries tried to make a go of it, but they never commercially caught on. There were a couple of beer bars, one being the Globe. When I acquired it in 2003, we had sixty beers. At that time, there were a few small importers bringing in product from Belgium, a few more British ales, but nothing from the States at all, apart from the big macros. And no local breweries. I started stocking some Aussie beers, including Coopers (which is close to my heart, for obvious reasons) and Little Creatures. Then a few Americans arrived in Hong Kong who were passionate about beer. They quickly realized that there was nothing from the States here, and they began importing some good American beers from Rogue, North Coast Brewing, Anderson Valley, and Anchor, to name a few. When this was well received, other importers came into the market. In 2010 or 2011, we began seeing an explosion of good beer in Hong Kong, abetted by a drop in the duties assessed on beer. There are now five good taprooms in the city and a handful

OPPOSITE:
*For publican
Toby Cooper, one
of the best places
to enjoy a local
beer in Hong
Kong is from the
deck of a junk
boat in Victoria
Harbour.*

DESTINATION 12

of other bars with a good beer selection. The Globe now carries a hundred and seventy beers, with twenty on tap. Six years ago, when I rebuilt the bar, there was very little good draft beer available. Now I wish I could have left room for more taps."

Some of those taps would have likely been reserved for the local brews that have emerged in the last few years. "Right now, there are eleven breweries operating in Hong Kong," Toby continued. "Some were started by expats, some by Hong Kong natives who've spent time overseas and came back with an interest in beer. The first new brewery is called Young Master and was started by a former banker. Young Master has been doing some great beers using local ingredients, and they've done a good job of attracting attention to local beer. One of their creations—Cha Chaan Teng Gose—is a German sour wheat beer made with salted lime. [Cha Chaan Teng translates to "tea restaurant"; salted lime is often served in the tea shops with lemon soda.] The Hong Kong Beer Company is also doing good work. The owners bought an existing brewery that was brewing very little (and not doing it very well) and hired a fantastic brewmaster, Simon Pesch (from Pyramid Breweries, Inc.). The other brewers are very small. Of the smaller players, I especially like Moonzen. It's a husband (from Mexico) and wife (local Chinese) team, and they brew in very small batches—their production is two thousand bottles a month. Their beers also use local ingredients and are fantastic; past creations have included a smoked plum ale and Szechuan pepper porter. Product from nanobreweries like Moonzen end up being expensive because of the scale of their operations. But in Hong Kong, there's not much price sensitivity. If people think something is good, they're willing to pay for it.

"Something else I'll say for the people of Hong Kong: They're very open-minded about trying new things. Perhaps because they don't have a history of a beer culture, they don't have a preconception about what beer should be. We have many younger people coming into the Globe in groups of five or six to do tastings. They are very eager to learn. They'll buy a few bottles of our big-format beers, share them, and talk about them the way people talk about wine. There's no beer snobbery. At least not yet."

Toby's efforts to spread the gospel of craft beer in Hong Kong found a fruitful collaboration with Jonathan So and Curt Schmidt, two entrepreneurs who launched Beertopia in 2012. "With Toby's guidance, we went to distributors who were hoping to find a market for some lesser known beers they'd imported," Curt recalled. "They were more than willing to pay for a stand to help sell their stock before it had degraded. We secured a venue, a few bands to play, launched a Facebook campaign, and hoped for the best. We needed at least a thousand people to attend to break even. Two thousand people showed up. The nice thing in Hong Kong is that if you create something unique, people will come out of curiosity. Beertopia didn't attract just beer lovers." The 2014 festival attracted over eleven thousand attendees and featured more than five hundred different beers from around the world.

Given Hong Kong's steamy subtropical climate, many bars and restaurants are geared toward allowing people to enjoy the outdoors. The Globe is a bit different. "We're in a basement, and we come into our own in the winter," Toby shared, "though it's not exactly an English winter. At this time, you can enjoy something big and cheery—like an imperial stout—which doesn't work so well in hot weather. But during the summer, I love to get out on Victoria Harbour. Taking a junk boat ride out to an island to swim and enjoy the beach is a Hong Kong recreational institution. A Cha Chaan Teng is a perfect accompaniment for a junk ride."

TOBY COOPER is the owner of the Globe, Hong Kong's best known beer bar. Having grown up in the north of England, he quickly realized the importance of good beer. After wandering around Asia and Australia for a few years, he washed up on Hong Kong's shores in 1996, never intending to stay. . .

If You Go

▶ **Getting There:** Hong Kong is served by most international carriers.

▶ **Best Time to Visit:** Many people prefer the cooler, drier weather of the winter season. The two-day Beertopia (www.beertopiahk.com) event is generally held in October.

▶ **Spots to Visit:** The Globe (+852 2543 1941; www.theglobe.com.hk); Young Master Ales (www.youngmasterales.com) and Moonzen Brewery (www.moonzen.hk) sometimes host open house events. The Beertopia website lists other craft beer bars around Hong Kong by neighborhood.

▶ **Accommodations:** Discover Hong Kong (www.discoverhongkong.com) lists a broad range of lodging options in the city.

DENVER

RECOMMENDED BY **Governor John Hickenlooper**

It was a strange confluence of circumstances—the self-reliance of Northern Mainers, a brief period of unemployment, and a house-building project in California—that collided to help make Denver the craft brewing capital of the Rockies.

"I spent some time in Maine's Washington County in the early seventies," Governor John Hickenlooper recalled. "It's a pretty poor part of the country, so everyone brewed their own beer, as it was so inexpensive. I learned to homebrew there; one of my creations was Hickenlooper Lager. If you couldn't say it, you weren't allowed to have another. Some years later, I found myself out in Denver. I was laid off from my job as a geologist. I bought a red Malibu convertible with my severance and drove out to Northern California to help my brother with a house project he was working on. This was 1986. One night, he took me out to a brewpub in Berkeley called Triple Rock. There was a line out the door on a Wednesday night. I remember thinking that I'd drive twenty miles out of my way to get beer like this . . . and that a concept like this could fly in Denver.

"I floated the idea to several people, and they were interested, but it never quite came together. So I went to the library and read a book on business plans and began looking for an older building to house the brewery. I wanted to do a pre-Prohibition kind of beer—just water, hops, yeast, and malt—and I wanted to put it in a pre-Prohibition building. I finally found one in LoDo [now one of Denver's hippest neighborhoods, but then considered Skid Row and in the early stages of redevelopment]. It took almost two years, but the brewpub—Wynkoop—opened in 1988. At the time, it was only the fourth brewery in Colorado [next to Coors, Anheuser-Busch, and Boulder Beer Company] and the first brewpub in the Rockies. It's still the largest brewpub in the world, at thirty-six thousand square feet. We were worried when other brewpubs began opening up, but it

OPPOSITE: The Great American Beer Festival is America's largest beer festival, with over seventy-five thousand visitors in attendance and three thousand beers flowing.

DESTINATION

13

soon became evident that Denver could support a lot of craft brewing. We had a lot of young people, and we have four seasons; each season calls for different kinds of beer, which attracts people with different tastes. I think all of us in the brewing world saw a kind of Häagen Dazs effect—people would be willing to spend more if they perceived a difference in quality."

Today, Denverites can opt for something a bit more spirited than a Coors Light (brewed just north in Golden) in more than forty craft breweries within the city limits. With less than 2 percent of America's population, Colorado accounts for over 10 percent of the nation's craft breweries—with the number (in 2015) approaching 250.

Visitors intent on exploring Denver's beer culture might begin with the two members of the old guard of Mile-High City brewing—Wynkoop and Great Divide. Wynkoop brews more than forty styles throughout the year (with roughly ten on tap at a given time) and boasts a second-floor billiards room with twenty-two pool tables. Their offerings run the gamut, from pale ales and IPAs to more adventurous offerings like Patty's Chile Beer (a golden ale fermented with Anaheim and ancho peppers) to Rocky Mountain Oyster Stout, which is flavored with . . . roasted bull testicles. Great Divide rests in Denver's Ballpark neighborhood. The brewery operates from an old dairy plant and pours sixteen beers at any given time from a portfolio of twenty-five varieties at its nearby taproom. Great Divide is one of the most decorated breweries in Colorado, with eighteen Great American Beer Festival medals and five World Beer Cup awards to its credit. John shared a few other spots worth a stop: "Epic Brewing [which originated in Salt Lake City] has twenty-five beers on tap at any time. Their flagship brew is a stout with a strong coffee profile. It's also worth stopping at Union Station [Denver's railroad depot]. The Terminal Bar [downstairs in the historic ticketing office] has a nice selection of craft beers, and you get a little taste of Denver's railroad history. If you enjoy live music, you have to visit Red Rocks Amphitheatre, just west of the city. The natural acoustics are amazing, and they hold one hundred concerts a year. You can find over a dozen craft beers there."

No mention of Denver as a beer-drinking destination would be complete without mention of the Great American Beer Festival, billed as the premier U.S. beer festival and competition. Each September, over six hundred brewers from all over the world gather at the Colorado Convention Center to share their wares and compete for prizes. Winners are determined by the GABF judge panel, which is made up of industry professionals from around the world. The panels conduct blind taste tests and select the three beers that best represent each beer-style category—a list that approaches 150 varieties! "If you want to try many, many different beers, you'll want to visit the GABF at some point," John added. "They've got three thousand beers flowing. It's America's biggest beer party, with seventy-five thousand visitors over three days."

GOVERNOR JOHN HICKENLOOPER was born in Pennsylvania. After earning a bachelor's degree in English and a master's degree in geology, both from Wesleyan University, he moved to Colorado in 1981, finding work with Buckhorn Petroleum. With the collapse of the oil industry in the 1980s, he was laid off and began life as a publican, opening the Wynkoop Brewing Company in 1988. In 2003, John was elected mayor of Denver. As mayor, he overhauled the city's financial system, created the city's first chief financial officer, and streamlined many city services. In 2005, after serving only two years as mayor, *Time* magazine placed him among the top five "big-city" mayors in the country. John ran for governor of Colorado in 2010 on a platform to make Colorado the best place for entrepreneurs to grow jobs. He won and was reelected in 2014. John is a devoted parent to his son and the proud owner of a rescue dog, Skye.

If You Go

▶ **Getting There:** Denver is served by most major carriers.

▶ **Best Time to Visit:** Denver attracts visitors year-round, be it for outdoor sports or the city's vibrant beer/food culture. The Great American Beer Festival (www.greatamerican beerfestival.com) is generally held the last weekend in September.

▶ **Spots to Visit:** Wynkoop Brewing Company (303-297-2700; www.wynkoop.com); Great Divide Brewing Company (303-296-9460; www.greatdivide.com); Epic Brewing Company (720-539-7410; www.epicbrewing.com); the Terminal Bar at Union Station (720-460-3701; www.terminalbardenver.com); Red Rocks Amphitheatre (720-865-2494; www.redrocksonline.com).

▶ **Accommodations:** The Denver Convention & Visitors Bureau (800-233-6837; www.denver.org) lists a broad range of lodging options in the Mile-High City.

TELLURIDE

RECOMMENDED BY **Steve Gumble**

A great pint of beer makes the best music sound even better. Add in some spectacular scenery, and you have the makings of a memorable weekend.

That's what you'll find each September in the mountain town of Telluride, Colorado, at the annual Telluride Blues & Brews Festival.

"Back in the early nineties, there was a wine festival in Telluride," Steve Gumble began. "My friends and I would go every year, drink copious amounts of wine, and talk about how it was time for Telluride to have a beer festival. By 1994, I decided I was going to do it. I owned a liquor store at the time and had some exposure to the emerging market of microbrews. I became friends with the guys who started New Belgium [in Fort Collins]. They were brewing out of their basement at the time, and they urged me to make the festival happen. Pretty soon, I was putting together a festival from the basement of my store. The first one was pretty easy to put together—a tent, some Porta-Pottys, donate the proceeds to charity. It was an overnight success and kept growing. We added a few bands. By 1997, we changed the name to the Blues & Brews Festival and moved the event to one of the most scenic music venues in the world—the Telluride Town Park."

Telluride is regularly voted one of the most beautiful towns in America; more than a few have driven into the historic downtown, looked about, and decided to relocate . . . whatever it took! It's hard to believe that into the early seventies, it was still mainly a mining town. The first ski lift went up in 1972. Several festivals (including the Telluride Bluegrass Festival) followed. As the area grew, it developed a "best-kept secret" reputation . . . which of course drew even more visitors. The mountains around Telluride were rumored to be a drop-off point for Mexican drug smugglers, and this burnished the town with a bit of a Wild West image; it was even featured in a song on the ubiquitous

OPPOSITE:
Quality music,
quality beer,
and impeccable
scenery come
together each
September at the
Telluride Blues
& Brews Festival.

cocaine-centric TV series *Miami Vice*, "Smugglers Blues" by the Eagles' Glen Frey. As more and more celebrities descended on the southwestern Colorado town, the counter-culture reputation gave way to one of rugged mountain chic. But limited development has helped reinforce the proposition of Telluride's tagline: "the most beautiful place you will ever ski."

Or attend a music festival.

The festival unfolds over three days in mid-September in Telluride Town Park, just as the leaves are beginning to take on their brilliant fall hues. (The town rests at 8,750 feet, so fall comes early!) Since its inauguration, the festival has attracted a veritable who's who of blues, funk, jam bands, rock, gospel, and soul performers. A short list of past performers includes Elvin Bishop, Gregg Allman, The Derek Trucks & Susan Tedeschi Band, Willie Nelson, Robert Cray, Mavis Staples, Gov't Mule, Little Feat, John Hiatt, George Clinton & Parliament Funkadelic, and James Brown. After the festival lights go down, many artists will continue playing at local bars. "It's hard to overstate just how beautiful the setting is," Steve continued. "Telluride is in a box canyon: the town park and the stage rest at one end, the other backs up to thirteen-thousand-foot mountain peaks and a waterfall. In fact, there are mountains on three sides. It's especially spectacular for the artists, as they're looking up at the mountains. When B. B. King first played here in 2004, he sat on the stage, looked out at the mountains and said 'Out of the ninety different countries I've been to, I've never seen anything more beautiful than what you have here.' If there's a bright sunset, there's tremendous alpenglow. You could have B. B. King on stage, but if the alpenglow is coming off, everyone is looking back. You never get tired of it."

While there is quality beer flowing throughout the festival (this year's fixed taps include products from Sierra Nevada, Bonfire Brewing, Durango Brewing Company, Ska Brewing, and Telluride Brewing Company), pouring reaches its peak on Saturday. "From twelve to three, we have the Grand Tasting," Steve explained. "Everyone who's purchased a show pass or single-day ticket gets a six-ounce glass. There are fifty-six breweries set up in tents throughout the park. There's an emphasis on Colorado brewers, but we have participants from as far away as Seattle and the Bay Area. Guests have three hours to taste as much or as little as they wish and can choose from over one hundred and seventy different beers. The music keeps playing throughout. I'm happy to say that our local brewery, Telluride Brewing Company, really holds its own with the offerings from around the state. I've watched it blossom into a major player in the region; they complement the festival and vice versa."

There have been many memorable moments for Steve Gumble at the event he helped create. But one festival that stands out is the 2001 event. "It was four days after 9/11, and James Brown was the headliner. He was adamant that he wanted to play, but trying to get him out here was a feat. We ended up leasing a private plane to get James and his band to Telluride; it was one of only a handful of jets in the air that weekend. He came out on stage wrapped in the American flag and closed with an a cappella version of 'God Bless America.' When Warren Haynes played, he closed the Saturday night show with Neil Young's 'Rockin' in the Free World.' I've never felt energy like that."

STEVE GUMBLE founded SBG Productions in 1994. The company specializes in multi-faceted live-music experiences, including the Snowmass Mammoth Fest in Snowmass, Colorado; the Durango Blues Train in Durango, Colorado; and the Telluride Blues & Brews Festival.

If You Go

▶ **Getting There:** The Montrose-Telluride area is served by Allegiant (702-505-8888; www.allegiantair.com), American (800-433-7300; www.aa.com), and Delta Airlines (800-221-1212; www.delta.com).

▶ **Best Time to Visit:** The Blues & Brews Festival (866-515-6166; www.tellurideblues.com) is generally held the third weekend in September.

▶ **Spots to Visit:** After the music is done, check out the following pubs: Telluride Brewing Company (970-728-5094; www.telluridebrewingco.com); Fly Me to the Moon Saloon (www.flymetothemoonsaloon.com); Smugglers Brewpub (970-728-5620; www.smugglers brewpub.com).

▶ **Accommodations:** Visit Telluride (888-605-2578; www.visittelluride.com) lists hotel options around town. Camping is available at the Blues & Brews site.

PRAGUE

RECOMMENDED BY **Peter Smith**

Prague, the romantic cultural center of central Europe, was established along the banks of the Vltava river in the year 885 AD . . . just a few years after the first recording of hops being cultivated in Bohemia. After all, Czechs began brewing beer for their own consumption at the turn of the *last* millenium. The pope frowned on brewing, but in the thirteenth century, King Wenceslas persuaded him to revoke anti-brewing ordinances . . . and commercial breweries soon followed. Today, Czechs consume more beer per capita than anyone else in the world (around forty gallons), and Prague boasts a rich brewing history and a bright future. (One theory on the popularity of beer among Czechs is that during the nation's Communist era, prices were kept artificially cheap to allow workers a simple and affordable pleasure. Though prices have risen, beer prices in the Czech Republic remain among the lowest in Europe.)

OPPOSITE:
Pilsner Urquell's brilliant golden color was a tremendous departure from murky beers available in the 1840s, and coincided with the introduction of glassware for mugs.

"Wandering around Prague the last ten years or so, you can smell hops and barley in the air," Peter Smith began. "There's also the aroma of fermenting beer. You didn't experience this fifteen years ago. Smaller breweries are coming back into prominence. Not so long ago, there were four or five beer choices that you found everywhere: Gambrinus, Staropramen, Budvar, Krušovice, and Pilsner Urquell. Now the market is more fractured, and there are many more choices. This has been in part a response to the market. Younger people are not automatically drinking beer, and brewers need to appeal to different tastes. That being said, you will never see a change to Pilsner Urquell. There are some places where you can get it unfiltered, some unpasteurized, but the recipe won't be changed."

The story of beer in the modern Czech Republic points to the town of Pilsen, about fifty miles southwest of the Czech capital. "Around the beginning of the thirteenth century, Pilsen happened to be positioned roughly halfway on the trade routes between Munich,

Vienna, and Prague," Peter explained. "It was a natural stopping-off point, and travelers wanted some relaxation—like beer. Thus, all the people who lived in Pilsen's main square were granted special rights to brew beer. They continued doing so until 1838. Over the years, it seems that the small brewers of Pilsen had been losing their edge. There was so much anger over the diminished quality of the beer, some of the city fathers took thirty-six barrels to the steps of the town hall and smashed them open in disgust. A year later, it was decided that brewers should join together to form one citizens' brewery to produce one great beer." The brewery was built, a Bavarian brewer named Josef Groll was retained to develop a better beer, and by 1842, the first kegs of what would come to be known as Pilsner Urquell were tapped to great acclaim. The original *pils*—a pale, bottom-fermented lager made with local Saaz noble hops—was a brilliant golden color, a tremendous departure from the darker, murkier beers of the day.

"Pilsner Urquell, poured fresh in Pilsen or Prague, has a distinct golden color like no other beer I've ever seen," Peter opined. "I think its immediate popularity had a good deal to do with the color. Glassware was introduced in the mid-nineteenth century to replace beer jugs and tankards. With glass, you couldn't have mucky looking beers. Today, there's variation in the quality of the pour. In my opinion, the best pour in Prague is at a place called Lokál. They have taken the old Czech idea of the beer cellar and modernized it. They do a perfect pour with the correct amount of head and have a great traditional menu that includes fried cheese served with potatoes, the classic Czech vegetarian dish. If you were to have only one beer in Prague, I would recommend it be a Pilsner Urquell at Lokál."

In general, Peter has seen a resurgence of beer halls in Prague. "Historically, Prague had the big German-style beer halls where people would gather and consume copious amounts of Gambrinus, Pilsner Urquell, and Staropramen. The halls went out of fashion during the Communist times. Though beer drinking was tolerated, the government wasn't thrilled about the idea of large groups of people congregating and drinking alcohol; there was concern this could foment demonstrations in Wenceslas Square. Now the beer halls are coming back. One that never went away is U Fleků, which dates back to 1499; I think it was just small enough to get past the Communists. They brew their own dark lager and have an oompah band in the evenings, which is great fun. U Pinkasů is another classic pub, just off Wenceslas Square. The first Pilsner Urquells were served here in 1843. In the early days, the beer was stored in the cellars but was served two stories up. The owner [Jakub Pinkas] demanded that the waiters make it from the bottom to the top as fast as possible so as not to compromise the quality of the beer. Once a year, the pub celebrates the old tradition with the U Pinkasů Nightmare, a forty-five-step run from the basement to the second floor, holding ten half-liter glasses full of beer."

Czech beer halls have sometimes been criticized for the inconsistent quality of their service; visitors to U Fleků, for example, may find slow or surly servers. But this is changing. "The beer halls and pubs are much cleaner, the food is better, and the atmosphere is less smoky. The beer has always been good. But now you can taste it."

PETER SMITH is a radio and TV journalist—both reporter and studio anchor—who's worked in China, Russia, the UK, and the Czech Republic. He began working in public relations and brand management a few years ago and is currently employed by Good Relations UK, working on accounts that include SABMiller and Centrica. Drawing heavily on his varied media experiences, Peter also provides corporate training seminars and coaching in interpersonal skills. His voice-over work has been featured in over 200 public and private films, documentaries, advertisements, and staff training videos.

If You Go

▶ **Getting There:** Prague is served from a number of European cities by a host of carriers. Delta (800-221-1212; www.delta.com) offers service from New York.

▶ **Best Time to Visit:** Summer sees the best weather and the most visitors; many enjoy Prague in the spring and fall, when the weather is still pleasant but the streets less crowded.

▶ **Spots to Visit:** Lokál (+420 222 316 265; www.lokal-dlouha.ambi.cz); U Fleků (+420 224 934 019; www.en.ufleku.cz); U Pinkasů (+ 420 221 111 152; www.upinkasu.com). Peter also recommends Prague Beer Museum (+420 732 330 912; www.praguebeer museum.com) to get a great overview of Prague's offerings. If you have an extra day, take the train to Pilsen (1.5 hours) and tour the Pilsner Urquell brewery (+420 377 062 888; www.prazdrojvisit.cz).

▶ **Accommodations:** Prague City Tourism (+420 221 714 714; www.prague.eu) lists a range of lodging options.

DESTINATION 15

THE COTSWOLDS

RECOMMENDED BY **James Blockley**

!

If there's a region that captures the quintessential look and feel summoned by the phrase "English countryside," it's the Cotswolds. Situated roughly two hours west of London, the Cotswolds are an achingly idyllic mix of rolling green hills, woods, and fields, dotted with quaint villages of yellow limestone and thatched-roof cottages. The villages of the Cotswolds are all connected by well-marked walking paths, which are in turn populated with fabulous country pubs. "One of the great appeals of the Cotswolds for me is its incredible variety," James Blockley began. "You can walk five miles along a well-groomed path and pass through incredible limestone grasslands, old-growth beech woodlands, and endless carpets of bluebells and find yourself in a sleepy village or thriving market town. All along the way, there are pubs that let you immerse yourself in the culture of each place. Walking and visiting pubs go together very well. Walking across a windy hilltop on a fall day to reach a friendly pub with a roaring fire—it's a marriage made in heaven. You feel like you've earned your pints."

The Cotswolds region stretches roughly ninety miles from Chipping Campden in the north to Bath in the south, with much of the area resting in the county of Gloucestershire. Though archaeological evidence suggests human settlement back to Neolithic times, the Cotswolds came to prominence for its sheep and thriving wool trade; there was a time when Cotswolds wool was considered the finest in the world. Sheep are still reared in the region, but it's better known today as a second-home retreat for wealthy Londoners and a destination for walkers. The Cotswold Way, one of fifteen designated national trails in England and Wales, winds 102 miles through the area; towns or villages are situated every eight or ten miles along the way, making for leisurely through-walking. Though some will walk the entire trail over several weeks (or several years, doing a section each year), many

OPPOSITE:
The Cotswolds have long been a walker's delight; fortunately, many of the region's paths have fine pubs along the way.

will choose to walk sections of the trail, or one of the many circular walks that connect villages on the Cotswold Way with outlying towns. In total, over three thousand miles of footpaths criss-cross the greater Cotswolds region.

For beer lovers, this is a very good time to be walking the winding paths of the Cotswolds. "There are so many microbreweries bang on the Cotswold Way," James continued. "Some are very new, doing more innovative beers—hop-forward IPAs, refreshing summer beers. Others focus on traditional brews—session ales, roughly four percent ABV. Wickwar brewery (in the village of Wickwar), for example, has been operating since the 1860s, but they've modernized and have taken on a new guise. Stanway Brewery is situated at the Stanway House, a manor house (near the town of Winchcombe) that dates back to Elizabethan times. The brewery had not been used for many years but is now operative again and is England's only wood-fired brewery; both coppers are heated with logs. Overall, the Cotswold brewing scene offers a great combination of old and new."

There are several strategies walkers can take to optimize both the Cotswolds' beautiful vistas and beer-tasting possibilities. "One tactic is to use a single village as a base and take a number of different walks from that spot," James explained. "There are enough different paths that you won't have to do the same walk twice. For example, you could base yourself in Winchcombe, near the northern end of Cotswold Way. There are many well-signed walking routes here. Just a bit north is one of our most beautiful walks, Snowshill to Stanton. When you reach Stanton, there's the Mount Inn. They have fantastic beer [brewed by Donnington Brewery], and being perched on a hill, have great views from their beer garden—on clear days all the way to Wales.

"What I generally recommend to visitors who really want to experience the region is to spend a night each in three or four different places. You might start out in Winchcombe and then head south to Painswick, which is roughly the halfway point along the Cotswold Way. Again, there are a number of fine walks from Painswick, and there's a wonderful pub there called the Edgemoor Inn. They have six or so great local ales available and sweeping views over the Painswick Valley. About two-thirds of the way down Cotswold Way is Wotton-under-Edge. It's a market town with some fine shops and one of my favorite pubs, the Star Inn. The pub dates back to the 1500s, and the story goes that the chap who started the White Star Line—the shipping company that built the Titanic—was born here. They serve a beer there called Cotswold Way. It's a beautiful chestnut-colored session ale, brewed just down the road at Wickwar, with good local water and a special strain of yeast. To me, it's the classic English pint, the Cotswolds in a glass. You can have a pint of Cotswold Way, and then walk it."

For James, no beer tour of the Cotswolds would be quite complete without a visit to Bath, where the quiet villages of the region give way to a vibrant small city that's been celebrated for its hot springs since 60 AD, when the Romans built the first baths here. "There's a pub called the Old Green Tree in Bath that's a two-minute walk from the end of Cotswold Way," James enthused. "They serve an ale called Old Green Tree that's made exclusively for them by Blindmans Brewery. Whether you've walked all the way from Chipping Campden to Bath or just around the block, you should stop at the Old Green Tree. If you've seen the Harry Potter movies, you'll see that the fictional Leaky Cauldron pub bears a striking resemblance."

JAMES BLOCKLEY is the trails and access officer for the Cotswolds Area of Outsanding Natural Beauty.

If You Go

▶ **Getting There:** The Cotswolds rest two hours west of London, which is served by major carriers. Train service (+44 20 7278 5240; www.nationalrail.co.uk) is available to Moreton-in-Marsh near the top of Cotswold Way; bus service is available from town to town.

▶ **Best Time to Visit:** The Cotswolds have a four-season charm. The Cotswold Beer Festival (www.gloucestershirecamra.org.uk), which features 150 real ales served on the grounds of a medieval estate near Cleeve Hill, is held at the end of July. For information about the many walking itineraries available, visit www.cotswoldsaonb.org.uk or www.nationaltrail.co.uk/cotswold.

▶ **Spots to Visit:** In Stanton, the Mount Inn (+44 01386 584316; www.themountinn.co.uk); in Painswick, the Edgemoor Inn (+44 1452 813576; www.edgemoorinn.com); in Wotton-under-Edge, the Star Inn (+44 1453 844651); in Bath, the Old Green Tree (+44 1225 448259).

▶ **Accommodations:** The Cotswolds website (www.cotswolds.com) lists a range of lodging options throughout the region.

LONDON

RECOMMENDED BY **Jezza**

"London has always had a fantastic assemblage of historical pubs, some very famous," Jezza began. "But for many years, these wonderful pubs didn't serve particularly good beer. Indeed, London had gained some notoriety as a place where you could reliably find a bad pint. Less than ten years ago, we reached a low point of less than ten breweries operating. Now there are eighty. The scene has exploded, both breweries and beer bars. Some of the old pubs have been transformed into modern beer bars."

Archaeological records show that beer has been consumed in what is now England since Roman times. It was commonly brewed at home through the Middle Ages, providing a safer alternative to water, and was also a means of storing calories. As in other northern brewing nations, the church eventually got into the action. (By the late 1200s, St. Paul's Cathedral is said to have produced some seventy thousand gallons of ale per annum.) But in 1342, the London Brewers' Guild formed, and laymen had begun taking control of the nascent brewing industry. Before the end of the century, there were three hundred commercial brewers in London. Beer was certainly part of daily life at Hampton Court Palace, Henry VIII's residence. It's believed that the king employed two brewers— one for beer and one for ale—and that thirteen thousand pints a day were produced, presumably making for a very merry court. The first pubs began appearing in London around this time. Ye Olde Mitre, which first opened its doors in Holborn in 1546, remains open today, as does The Prospect of Whitby (established 1520) in Wapping.

Over the next three or four hundred years, London saw consolidation among its brewing interests and the introduction of several standard-bearing styles—most notably, porter, the first mass-produced beer, named after the working-class drinkers who popularized the dark ale. By the early 1970s, several brewing conglomerates controlled much of

OPPOSITE:
London was
once known
for fine pubs
pouring terrible
beer, but modern
establishments
like Brewdog are
changing that
perception.

production in the United Kingdom, and taste and quality declined. A small group of imbibers—Michael Hardman, Graham Lees, Jim Makin, and Bill Mellor—decided that British beer drinkers deserved better and formed the Campaign for the Revitalization of Ale (CAMRA; later known as Campaign for Real Ale). CAMRA rallied support for traditional ales and more eclectic brewers and eventually became recognized as Europe's most successful consumer campaign, with nearly 165,000 members. Many early American craft brewers cite the Real Ale movement as inspiration for their work. (Technically speaking, "real ale" is defined as cask-conditioned ale, delivered to your pint glass via hand-pulls.)

"Some people in the beer community get very exercised about the definition of real ale and are concerned that some of the newer beers are being served in kegs, rather than casks," Jezza continued. "Personally I'm more concerned that it's good beer, rather than the format it comes in. There are easily two hundred places serving great beer now in London, a majority of them new. A case in point: in 2014, we had a few beer-loving friends visiting from Austin who had last visited in 2003. Over three days, we took them on a tasting tour that included twenty-six pubs and bars. Not one of the twenty-six spots was open eleven years before. In terms of styles, London brewers are offering a hugely eclectic mix. There are a number of trends emerging. One is recipes with large quantities of hops, many pale ales, and IPAs . . . some more successful than others. Many brewers are experimenting with Belgian yeast and brewing untraditional English styles—saisons, Berliner weisse, for example. Porters are also seeing a resurgence, a nod to London brewing history. The best time to get an overview of the range of quality beers is in mid-August during London Beer City (a week of beer events in August) and the London Craft Beer Festival."

It is one thing to sample the flavors of the London beer renaissance, but most visitors will also wish to get a taste of the city's vibrant pub and beer bar culture. Given the veritable explosion of new beer bars, the potential for new crawls is dizzying. Jezza shared one adventure he recently assembled, the Central Line crawl. "The Central Line crawl offers five venues with a staggering total of over one hundred and twenty taps, plus around three hundred bottled beers. All can be accessed from one tube line. And all but one have opened since late 2013. You'll start near the Bethnal Green station, where there are two excellent stops nearby—Mother Kelly's and Redchurch Brewery taproom. Mother Kelly's has twenty-three draft beers in an airy, arched room. Redchurch offers ten of the brewery's offerings on tap. It's a bit more minimalist than Mother Kelly's. Next, you'll ride down to St. Paul's station and walk over to Harrild and Sons, which has a quirky design with huge mirrors and exposed brick. They offer a good range of cask and keg options, and one of the standout bottled-beer lists in London, with nearly one hundred choices. Now, you'll continue west on the Central Line to Tottenham Court and Craft Beer Co. They have the largest draft selection in London, with forty-five taps (fifteen casks, thirty kegs). It's a comfortable spot, and may be difficult to leave, but you'll want to finish the crawl by heading west to Shepherd's Bush station and BrewDog. The Shepherd's Bush pub is the third London BrewDog location and offers forty taps, half of which are usually BrewDog beers. BrewDog's great bar staff tops off the experience."

Should you find yourself near the City of London (the financial center), consider a stop at an older-guard establishment, the Counting House (established 1893). "It's opposite the Bank of England and is run by Fuller's, one of the oldest breweries in London," Jezza described. "They're still doing brilliant traditional cask beers."

JEZZA is a southwest London–based beer writer. A frequent beer traveler to Belgium and the United States, he's recently found he doesn't have to travel so far for good beer. Jezza's focus is now on the London beer scene; his guide to London's pubs and breweries is at www.beerguideldn.com. Follow Jezza on Twitter: @BeerGuideLondon.

If You Go

▶ **Getting There:** London is served by most international carriers.
▶ **Best Time to Visit:** The London Craft Beer Festival (www.londoncraftbeerfestival.co.uk) is held each year in mid-August.
▶ **Spots to Visit:** Mother Kelly's (+44 0 20 7012 1244; www.motherkellys.co.uk); Redchurch Brewery (+44 0 20 3487 0255; www.theredchurchbrewery.com); Harrild and Sons (+44 0 20 3714 2497; www.harrildandsons.com); Craft Beer Co. (www.thecraftbeerco.com); BrewDog (www.brewdog.com); the Counting House (+44 0 20 7283 7123; www.the-counting-house.com).
▶ **Accommodations:** Visit London (www.visitlondon.com) lists a host of lodging options.

PARIS

RECOMMENDED BY **Camille Malmquist**

It's safe to say that beer has historically had a bit of an image problem in France. But that is changing.

"Traditionally, beer has been viewed as a lower-class drink," Camille Malmquist began. "It was something that a butcher might drink after unloading his market haul, or a beverage people might have while watching a soccer match. Beer was not considered a good-taste experience; it was something to quench your thirst. Given the kind of industrial beers that were available, that's not surprising. In recent years, French people have been traveling outside of France with greater frequency and tasting beer from other places. They've had the realization that beer can have character and taste. The French are very interested in eating and drinking well. Once the word got out that there are good beers out there, they were interested. You can see this trend in Paris. A few years ago, if you wanted to drink anything with character, you had to be content with an import from Belgium. There are now a number of bars that focus on craft beer from farther afield and from France. And they are packed every night."

While beer may not have a rich pedigree in the gustatory annals of France, it has a robust history. There were nearly three thousand small breweries operating here in the early 1900s; presumably, it wasn't only butchers and soccer fans who enjoyed quaffing a beer now and again! France's small brewers were slowly subsumed by larger enterprises or chose to close their doors. Distinctive taste fell victim to consolidation, and by the mid-1970s, fewer than thirty breweries were operating in France, most cranking out lackluster lagers. These were perhaps best typified by Kronenbourg, France's primary beer export to the United States. France is certainly known for its many grape-growing regions, but you may not realize that a great deal of barley is grown here, the

OPPOSITE:
Paris, the city of light, of romance, and, increasingly, of beer!

raw material for malt. In fact, France is Europe's largest barley producer and the world's greatest exporter of malt. Some are now staying closer to home. "One brewer I know, an American named Mike Donohue, wanted to set up shop in Paris," Camille continued, "because he wanted to source all of his ingredients as locally as possible. Here, he can get both barley and hops from nearby."

The brewery that Donohue started with Thomas Deck, a Frenchman that he met years before at Georgetown University, is representative of the new breed of Parisian brewers. Donohue and Deck started out home brewing while living in San Francisco. Deck returned to France, and Donohue remained in the States and learned the brewing trade. Some ten years after their first meeting, both men quit their jobs, Donohue moved to Paris, and they opened up Deck & Donohue in the Montreuil neighborhood, brewing both American styles (like Mission Pale Ale and Indigo IPA) as well as saisons and brown ales. "On Saturdays, Deck & Donohue open up their workshop to visitors," Camille said. "I was there on one occasion when Garrett Oliver from Brooklyn Brewery was visiting. The brewing community is very strong, and it was great fun to be surrounded by people who are interested in beer."

Paris may not have quite caught up to Portland, Oregon or Munich in terms of beer-drinking venues, but it seems that new spots are coming online each month. Camille shared a few of her regular stops. "Express de Lyon is one of my favorites. You wouldn't recognize it as a craft beer place. It's a little corner bar like many you'll find in France. Most such establishments have a big TV and betting on horse races—kind of depressing, really. But this place is very convivial, and they have fifteen amazing beers on tap. It's a craft beer bar in disguise. Les Trois 8 is a bit out of the way on the east side of Paris—in what Fox News would refer to as the 'no go' zone. The 'three eights' refers to the three shifts in a factory. Les Trois 8 is a grungy, rock-and-roll bar that would have felt at home in Seattle in the nineties. They have a good selection of both draft and bottled craft beers. La Fine Mousse is considered the granddaddy of craft beer bars in Paris. They have the city's biggest selection, twenty-one taps, all craft. Le Supercoin is unique in that they feature only French craft beer, they offer some of the cheapest craft beer in Paris—€3.50 or €4 for a half pint [technically .25 liters]. That's one thing you should know about ordering beer in France; it's generally served in a metric half pint unless you request otherwise. In terms of styles, we're seeing many IPAs and their ilk, as well as many sour beers.

"Brewpubs are not a big part of the scene as of now, though that's slowly changing. One true French gastrobrewpub is Le Triangle. It's a tiny space. The brewer is from Quebec, his wife runs the dining room, and her brother, a former Four Seasons chef, runs the kitchen. They have eight taps, with two to four house brews."

Some Americans shy away from visiting Paris, fearing their bad (or complete lack of) French will render them outcasts. This is a misconception; Parisians are generally quite tolerant of nonfluent speakers, and you'll find an especially inviting atmosphere among beer lovers. "In the beer bars, it's very easy to start conversations," Camille added. "You might start chatting with the bartender about the beers on tap, and you'll end up chatting with others and making friends—beer geek to beer geek."

CAMILLE MALMQUIST is a pastry chef who has worked in restaurants, bakeries, and pastry shops both in Paris and the United States. She has written for *Secrets of Paris* and *Girls' Guide to Paris*, and wrote the dessert and bun recipes for *Hamburger Gourmet* (Marabout, 2012). A native of the Pacific Northwest, Camille has been a fan of craft beer since before she could afford to drink it. She's been seeking out good beer in France since her arrival in 2008. She posts beer reviews, cooking tips, recipes, and travel stories on her blog, *Croque-Camille*, and ideas for seasonal cooking on its little sibling, *Seasonal Market Menus*.

If You Go

▶ **Getting There:** Orly and Charles de Gaulle Airports are served by most major carriers, including Air France (www.airfrance.com).

▶ **Best Time to Visit:** Cooler months are a great time to gather in a pub, though summer visitors will enjoy a picnic with a bottle of good beer from one of Paris's bottle shops.

▶ **Spots to Visit:** Express de Lyon (+33 01 43 43 21 32; www.expressdelyon.blogspot.fr); Les Trois 8 (+33 01 40 33 47 70; www.lestrois8.fr); La Fine Mousse (+33 09 80 45 94 64; www.lafinemousse.fr); Le Supercoin (www.supercoin.net); Le Triangle (+33 1 71 39 58 02).

▶ **Accommodations:** The French Tourist Office (www.francetourism.com) lists a broad assortment of lodging options.

BERLIN

RECOMMENDED BY **Marcel Krueger**

Perhaps no city in the world is more celebrated for its cultural trendsetting than Berlin. For more than a century, artists, gay people, and others that didn't quite fit in at home have found acceptance in this tolerant capital of Germany. This has led to an outpouring of creativity that spans from architecture to design to a thumping late-night club scene that's likely to leave the most hardened New York club kid blushing.

But beer? Not so much.

"When I first left Germany for Ireland in 2006," Marcel Krueger began, "much of Germany was still in the hands of the big brands. In the south of the country this wasn't always the case. But elsewhere, even in small pubs in the middle of nowhere, your options were all lager-based—Beck's, Warsteiner, sometimes even Heineken. Ireland was the same way at first—Guinness and Kilkenny, and not many alternatives in between. But before I left Ireland to move back to Germany in 2012, craft brewing had begun to pick up. When I arrived in Berlin that year, I didn't expect much . . . and I wasn't disappointed. Berlin doesn't really have the pub culture as you'd know it from Ireland or the United Kingdom. There are fancy new bars geared toward hipsters, or longstanding corner bars that seem geared toward alcoholics looking for a lager and a shot at ten in the morning.

"I live in a neighborhood of Berlin called Wedding. It's an older, blue-collar area, with high unemployment, a large Turkish community, kebab shops, and cheap gambling halls. In 2012, I learned that it was also the home of Berlin's only craft brewery, Eschenbräu—though that term wasn't even being used. They just called it a local brewery. It's certainly nothing fancy. The brewing facility has three seven-hundred-liter brew kettles. The main taproom is in the basement of a 1980s housing estate, more resembling a large rumpus

OPPOSITE:
Berlin may
not have the
beer pedigree
of Bavaria, but
newcomers drawn
by the city's
vibrant culture
are creating
a new, local
beer scene.

room in a youth center more than a cozy pub. But it attracts both locals and beer lovers from all across Berlin."

While Berlin may not have the beer pedigree of Munich, it *is* part of Germany . . . and as such, has a brewing tradition that would make many other cities proud. "You see, Berlin is a very flat city," Marcel continued. "The one natural hill here is in Prenzlauer Berg. The hill was the only place where people could fashion rock cellars for fermentation, so many of the breweries—some forty or fifty—were here. Brewing was very much a neighborhood activity then. Each neighborhood had their own brewer. Residents knew him and where his beer could be bought. Small brewers began to be bought out toward the end of the nineteenth century. After World War II, only a few bigger brewers were left, including Schultheiss. Before reunification, they operated on both sides of the Iron Curtain; you could buy a capitalist Schultheiss or a communist Schultheiss." (Today, one of the old Schultheiss breweries serves as a culture center—or, as it's known in Berlin, a *Kulturbrauerei*, or "Culture Brewery.")

Many of Berlin's new breed of brewers have materialized from elsewhere. Their product is finding many happy consumers. "There has been concern about gentrification in Berlin," Marcel opined, "about newcomers pushing out local residents. But the new people are also bringing energy and money into downtrodden areas. And they're making beer, something we can understand. I think part of the attraction is the appeal of local products. Commercially brewed beer that's not made according to the German purity law (*Reinheitsgebot*) cannot be sold as beer, so the brews are called by their English names— stout, pale ale, etc. Some of the local beers are replacing the bigger brands, even in the corner bars. Restaurants are popping up with beer themes. There's one that serves only pancakes and beer—another barbecue and beer. The brewers I know are very unpretentious about their craft. They just want to make good beer, with local ingredients if possible. They are very community-based."

If there was any question that beer insiders are beginning to take notice of the Berlin scene, San Diego's hop-forward Stone Brewing will open a location in Berlin in 2016.

In addition to visiting Eschenbräu, those interested in sampling the Berlin beer scene should plan to visit Vagabund and Bierfabrik. "Vagabund is in my Wedding neighborhood and was opened by three Americans," Marcel shared. "It was the first successfully crowd-funded brewery in Europe. They serve their own beers, as well as some Belgian ales and lagers from family brewers in the south of Germany. When they were building the brewery, most of the neighbors were positive, but one older lady gave them the evil eye. They didn't understand why she was negative. Then she heard they were building a brewery and was friendly. It turned out the space used to be used by the Hell's Angels motorcycle gang for a money-laundering operation, and she thought the Americans might be doing the same thing. Bierfabrik was started in a former animal-auction area, Börse Marzahn. It's adjacent to a gallery—Hilbert Raum—and some of the gallery's art hangs in the brewery.

Berlin's infamous club culture and the world of craft brewing do not often comingle. "You wouldn't go to a club to enjoy a nice beer," Marcel advised. "They usually don't serve it. But there is a club near Bierfabrik called Czar Hagestolz. When Bierfabrik launches a new beer, they sometimes do it at the club. One of their beers, Rummelsnuff's Kraftbock, is inspired by a musician named Rummelsnuff. He is a body builder, and the strong beer (9 percent ABV) is linked with his strong image."

MARCEL KRUEGER is a writer, translator, and editor who owns a sword cane and a laptop. He frequently writes about history, travel, or booze and was once called an "adventurer" by a Russian newspaper. Marcel's essays and stories have been published in the *Daily Telegraph*, *Reykjavik Grapevine*, and *Süddeutsche Zeitung*, among others. Marcel divides his time between Berlin and Dublin. He likes heavy metal and is afraid of spiders. You can find some of his work at www.kingofpain.org.

If You Go

▶ **Getting There:** Berlin is served by most major international carriers.
▶ **Best Time to Visit:** The International Berlin Beer Festival (www.bierfestival-berlin.de) is held in early August each year.
▶ **Spots to Visit:** Eschenbräu (+49 0162 493 1915; www.eschenbraeu.de); Vagabund (+49 030 5266 7668; www.vagabundbrauerei.com); Bierfabrik (+49 30 91456864).
▶ **Accommodations:** Visit Berlin (+49 030 25 00 23 33; www.visitberlin.de) lists lodging options throughout the city.

MUNICH

RECOMMENDED BY **Stefan Hempl**

In recent years, there have been a number of upstarts laying claim to the sobriquet Beer Capital of the World. Arrivistes may come and go, but given its pedigree, its abundance of breweries old and new, and a little festival locals know as the Wiesn, it's pretty hard to displace Munich as the reigning king of beer.

"The Munich beer scene is very old and traditional," began Stefan Hempl. "One of the breweries that's still operating, Augustiner-Bräu, has been brewing since 1328. The scene is dominated by six big brewers—Hofbräuhaus, Löwenbräu, Spaten, Paulaner, and Hacker-Pschorr, in addition to Augustiner-Bräu—and their famous beer halls. But there are also almost two hundred beer gardens in Munich, including Hirschgarten, which can accommodate eight thousand people. And of course, there's the Oktoberfest."

Munich, the capital of the state of Bavaria in the southeastern corner of Germany, dates back nearly a thousand years. It was here, in 1447, that the city council enacted an ordinance demanding the use of only barley, hops, and water in the production of beer; this would later become known as the *Reinheitsgebot*, or Bavarian beer-purity law, in 1516. (It was later expanded to all of Germany; yeast was not included in the list of ingredients, as it had not yet been discovered.) A number of beer styles have held sway in Munich over the centuries. Though dunkel beers (a dark, malty lager) were long the most popular style, helles and weissbier have supplanted it in popularity in more recent times. Where to enjoy Munich's fine lagers, rather than what to enjoy, is the larger question visitors face. One would not do badly to begin with a stop at a few of the big six. Hofbräuhaus is high on most lists. Established in 1589 by Duke Wilhelm V (though its present building has only been in existence since 1897), Hofbräu departs from the weissbier norm, boasting a darker beer, known as maibock (or, more commonly, bock) as its flagship brew. Ask

OPPOSITE:
Some of
the fourteen
"big tents" at
Oktoberfest can
accommodate
more than
10,000 revelers
at any given time.

a Münchner where the heart of the city's beer culture resides, and they'd likely say in Munich's many beer gardens. The gardens originally developed as cooling cover for beer cellars built along the Isar river in the nineteenth century. Guests sit at communal picnic tables, and beer is often served from wooden barrels in a Maßkrug, a liter-size glass mug. Guests can bring in their own food or purchase victuals onsite. A few of the most popular include Chinesischer Turm, Augustiner-Keller, Hofbräukeller, and Löwenbräukeller.

Munich's ancient beer halls and sprawling Biergärtens are central to the Bavarian beer and cultural experience, but no event speaks to the region—or to beer—like Oktoberfest. A few statistics speak to the sobering magnitude of the event: In 2013, some 6.4 million attendees over two weeks consumed nearly 1.8 million gallons of beer. If you're looking to sip a few quiet pints with a good friend, Oktoberfest may not be your style. Oktoberfest had considerably more modest roots: it began as a celebration of the union of Crown Prince Ludwig I to Princess Therese (of Saxony-Hildburghausen) in October of 1810 on the fields in front of the city gates. (These fields became known as Theresienwiese, or "Therese's fields"; the abbreviation of Theresienwiese, Wiesn, is now shorthand for the celebration.) The event ended with a series of horse races, and it was decided that the races would be held again the following year . . . and a tradition was established. Small beer stands were established by 1818 to slake the thirst of attendees, who could also ride a carousel or one of two swings. By 1896, the modest stands had been replaced by beer tents and halls, complete with the backing of major brewers . . . and the future template was set.

Today's Oktoberfest is spread over more than one hundred acres. There are fourteen big tents, twenty smaller tents, and a variety of other attractions. (Big is not an overstatement—the Winzerer Fähndl tent can accommodate more than ten thousand revelers between its inside and outside areas!) Stefan filled in some of the details: "The scope of the Oktoberfest tents is so great, construction begins in July; it takes nearly three months to put everything up. Every beer that is sold during the festival is brewed according to the *Reinheitsgebot*, and the styles served are very similar. The Oktoberfest beer is a Märzen style; most are 6 percent ABV by volume. The beer from one brewer might be a bit more malty, one might have more pronounced hops—but they are pretty uniform. Some people may forget that the beer has a higher alcohol content than lighter lagers. The food of Bavaria is a great attraction and helps people keep their balance. There will be half chickens, a variety of sausages, spare ribs, pork knuckles, and of course, spätzle.

"The beginning of the Oktoberest (on the third Saturday in September) is always special. Representatives from all the breweries parade through the center of Munich with horses and carts and bands. Everyone is wearing traditional clothes. No beer can be served until the mayor of Munich taps the first keg at noon the first day in the Schottenhamel tent. The mayor cries '*O'zapft is!*' ('It's tapped!') and serves the first mug of beer to the minister of Bavaria. Then kegs are tapped in other tents, and the beer begins to flow. On the first Sunday, people take to the streets in traditional Bavarian clothes—lederhosen for men, dirndls for females—to dance and sing. You have the sense that every citizen of Munich is there. It used to be just Bavarian people who dressed up this way, but now if you see a guy in lederhosen, he might be Japanese or Italian.

"The beer, the food, the music are all wonderful. But what I like most about Oktoberfest is the party atmosphere where you can get to know lots of people. If you can't find friends at Oktoberfest, something is wrong!"

STEFAN HEMPL was born in Munich and has lived there all his life. Since 1997 he has worked for Hofbräu München, where he now serves as the brewery's Press Officer and the spokesman of the Hofbräu Festival tent at the Oktoberfest.

If You Go

▶ **Getting There:** Munich is served by most international carriers.

▶ **Best Time to Visit:** Oktoberfest begins on the third Saturday in September and runs through the first Sunday in October.

▶ **Spots to Visit:** The official Oktoberfest website (www.oktoberfest.de) has all the details you need to plan your visit. If you visit at another time of year—or want to get away from the tents—consider Hofbräuhaus (+49 89 290136-10; www.hofbraeuhaus.de); Chinesischer Turm (+49 89 3838730; www.chinaturm.de); Augustiner-Keller (+49 89 594393; www.augustinerkeller.de); Hofbräukeller (+49 89 4599250; www.hofbraeuke ller.de); Löwenbräukeller (+49 89 54726690; www.loewenbraeukeller.com).

▶ **Accommodations:** The Oktoberfest website (www.oktoberfest.de) also details lodging options for Oktoberfest visitors.

DESTINATION 20

ISLAND PARK

RECOMMENDED BY **Amelie Kappes**

The pastime of fly fishing is generally considered an individual sport in the extreme. "Many think of the sport as a soulful, solo thing," Amelie Kappes began. "You do have to be extremely focused to have success. But at Henry's Fork, you're immersed in a very social, very like-minded community. Fly fishing becomes a group-oriented activity. Every fish that's caught is discussed in detail at the boat take-out, at dinner, and at the bar."

And that story is frequently accompanied by a cold beer.

Idaho's Henry's Fork is arguably the most famous trout stream in the world. It bubbles up from Big Springs, to the west of Yellowstone National Park, and meanders some 120 miles in a generally southerly direction before joining the Snake River southwest of the town of Rexburg. En route, it flows through steep canyons, across plateaus with sweeping views of the Centennial Mountains to the west and the Tetons to the east, and over tumultuous waterfalls. The area is home to many of the animals that you'd expect to find in Yellowstone—grizzlies, moose, pronghorn antelope, cougar, elk, and wolves . . . though most come in hopes of encountering the Henry's rainbow trout. The fish are not native to the river (they were first stocked in the late 1800s), but the Henry's mineral-rich waters sustain a wide variety of aquatic insects that, in turn, sustain good numbers of very large trout. Fish over twenty-four inches are commonly encountered, and the thrill of hooking and landing such a fish on a fly that's smaller than your pinkie nail is one of fly fishing's life-list accomplishments.

"I grew up fishing with my parents on the Feather River in the foothills of California's Sierra Nevadas," Amelie continued. "You could flick any fly into the water and catch a small trout. I really learned to fly fish when I came up to the Henry's Fork. I had been working in the financial-services industry in San Francisco after college, and a few years

OPPOSITE:
Celebratory beers
will have to wait
until the evening
hatch is done
on the Henry's
Fork, perhaps
the world's
most celebrated
trout stream.

of that wore me to the ground. I knew the owner of Henry's Fork Lodge (Nelson Ishiyama) from the city, and he suggested I come up to work at the lodge for a summer. It became my happy place. I met my husband (then a fly-fishing guide) there and built a house. I live in the Bay Area now, but Henry's Fork is still the place where I go to unwind and reflect on what's important. Once you get to the level where you can catch fish here, it's hard not to fall in love with the sport of fly fishing."

If there's one section of river that engages the collective fly-fishing imagination, it would probably be the nine miles flowing through Harriman State Park, known to some as "the Railroad Ranch" or simply "the Ranch." (The land adjoining the river through this stretch was donated to the state of Idaho by the Harriman family, which made its fortune in the railroad industry.) The waters of the Ranch flow slowly, with many subtle micro-currents. When insects begin appearing on the surface, onlookers may notice ringlets or snouts appearing above the water . . . and anglers will scramble to present their flies. Given the Henry's reputation, these flies are likely not the first that the trout have seen. The experience of drifting flies past indifferent trout can be humbling, frustrating, if not downright maddening. But that's part of the Henry's perverse appeal.

A favorite place to discuss the day's travails—and even observe other anglers at work in the fading twilight—is the deck of the TroutHunter Lodge, in the tiny settlement of Island Park. The TroutHunter rests near the top of the Ranch section; the Henry's sacred waters are just a few casts' lengths away from the deck, and the Centennials rise in the distance. "The TroutHunter is the most fun place to enjoy after-fishing beers in Island Park," Amelie opined. "This is where all the guides and fisher people gather to swap tales about the day's angling. There might be moose coming down to the river to drink, bald eagles flying overhead, or osprey dive-bombing fish. If there are any snouts popping up, onlookers might grab a rod and make a few casts." Beer aficionados will have a number of good choices. Island Park is at the nexus of Wyoming, Idaho, and Montana, and sur-rounding outdoor recreation hubs—Jackson, Big Sky, Bozeman, and Driggs—produce fine beers. "Bozeman Brewing does Montana Common [a California steam-style lager] and Hopzone IPA," Amelie added. "I like KettleHouse's [out of Missoula] Double Haul IPA. Lone Peak [from Big Sky] does a fine stout. And the beers from Grand Teton and Snake River Brewing [Driggs and Jackson, respectively] are quite good. If you want to buy some beers for lunch on the river, my favorite turnout place is the Grub Stake."

After a few days matching wits with the Henry's rainbows, you might desire a little break from the happy crowds at the TroutHunter. Henry's Fork Lodge, a few miles down the road, is the perfect respite. "The lodge is removed from the road and sits high above a section of the river just below the Ranch," Amelie described. "It's more of an upscale and intimate dining experience. A beer on the back porch, sitting in a rocking chair looking out on the river, is part of the ritual, before dinner . . . or after."

AMELIE KAPPES is the General Manager at Henry's Fork Lodge in Island Park, Idaho. She is responsible for the overall leadership of the lodge during the fishing season (late May through early October) and works from the San Francisco office during the rest of the year. Before joining the Henry's Fork Lodge and Ishiyama Corporation, Amelie worked as an Associate Relationship Manager at RCM Capital Management, a subsidiary of Allianz Global Investors, in San Francisco. She was also the Preserve Manager at The Nature Conservancy's Flat Ranch in Island Park, Idaho, for two years. Amelie earned degrees in Journalism and Mass Communication from University of Colorado, Boulder, and Agriculture with a specialization in Soil Science from Cal Poly San Luis Obispo.

If You Go

▶ **Getting There:** Last Chance, Idaho, is approximately 120 miles south of Bozeman and sixty miles north of Idaho Falls. Both are served by several carriers, including Allegiant Air (702-505-8888; www.allegiantair.com); Delta (800-221-1212; www.delta.com); and United (800-864-8331; www.united.com).

▶ **Best Time to Visit:** Mid-June to July is considered the peak season, though some prefer fall, as the river is less crowded.

▶ **Spots to Visit:** TroutHunter (208-558-9900; www.trouthunt.com) for a beer with the angling crowd; Henry's Fork Lodge (208-558-7953; www.henrysforklodge.com) for a more low-key dinner and post-dinner beer. Grub Stake (208-558-7209) if you desire a few beers for the river.

▶ **Accommodations:** TroutHunter and Henry's Fork Lodge both offer a number of packages for visiting anglers.

MIDDLE FORK OF THE SALMON RIVER

RECOMMENDED BY **Ken Grossman**

The label of Sierra Nevada's flagship brew, Sierra Nevada Pale Ale, depicts a blue river flowing forth from distant snow-capped mountains. It underscores the importance of clean water if you're trying to brew beer, while transporting the viewer to a bucolic water-side setting. Given the pale ale label—and that water graces many Sierra Nevada labels—it should come as no surprise that one of Sierra Nevada founder Ken Grossman's favorite places to enjoy a fine brew is along the banks of a river: Idaho's Middle Fork of the Salmon.

"I've always had a real affinity for the mountains and wild places in general," Ken began. "I've been a backpacker since I was a young man, and my hiking took me along many rivers. I suppose that fostered a connection to rivers, though I didn't become interested in white-water rafting until much later. In the last few years, I've done several extended river trips. The Middle Fork stands out for its beauty and sense of isolation."

The Middle Fork of the Salmon carves its way 106 miles through the second-largest wilderness areas in the United States—the 2.4-million-acre Frank Church–River of No Return Wilderness—in the heart of central Idaho.

White-water enthusiasts love it for its more than three hundred rapids, including infamous runs like Velvet Falls, Pistol Creek, Tappan Falls, Haystack, Hell's Half Mile, Powerhouse, Weber, and Rubber. Fly anglers love it for its freely rising cutthroat trout. And infrequent outdoors people—including presidents and other assorted potentates—embrace it as a place where they can immerse themselves in one of the last great wilderness areas left in the Lower 48.

Rafters generally stage in the town of Stanley, are shuttled to the put-in at Boundary Creek, and then float the river over the course of six days/five nights to the take-out below the Middle Fork's confluence with the main stem of the Salmon. In its upper reaches, at

OPPOSITE:
The Middle Fork
of the Salmon
River offers one
of the world's
great white-water
experiences . . .
abetted by jockey
boxes filled with
Sierra Nevada's
finest.

an elevation near seven thousand feet, the Middle Fork is an intimate, high-gradient stream, hemmed in closely by thick forests of Douglas fir and spruce. As you proceed downriver, the canyon opens up to expose jaw-dropping crags of Idaho Batholith that climb to the sky. The area is home to elk, deer, moose, mountain lions, and black bears, though these critters are seldom encountered, as they summer higher in the mountains. Bighorn sheep and mountain goats, however, are often seen cavorting on the cliffsides. Several natural hot springs present themselves along the river; Sunflower Showers, a hot spring that includes natural pools and a makeshift shower, is especially nurturing for sore paddling or casting shoulders.

A couple Oregonians—Buzz Hatch and Woody Hindman—began running the Middle Fork in the 1940s in McKenzie-style drift boats, and word started getting out about the wonders of the river. Today there are twenty-four outfitters licensed to escort guests down the Middle Fork, though only a handful of outfitters are allowed to launch each day. This preserves the quality of the river experience; you're not shoulder to shoulder with fellow rafters. While a few intrepid rowers take to the river in drift boats, most are in sturdy inflatable rafts, which are much more forgiving if you happen to bump into rocks . . . which in some of the Middle Fork's rapids is almost a fait accompli.

"When we did the Middle Fork trip, we dragged a dozen five-gallon kegs of various Sierra Nevada ales along for the group," Ken recalled. "We wanted to have a hoppy ale and a milder ale available each evening. I think the outfitters were a little surprised at the amount of beer that we dragged along, but they were ready. We had these super-insulated jockey boxes to keep the cold beer flowing. At one point we ran low on ice, but fortunately we were able to do an ice run at a dude ranch that's along the river." (Jockey box coolers, if you're unfamiliar with the idea, employ either aluminum "cold plates" or stainless steel coils to cool beer down. It runs from the keg—with the help of a CO_2 cartridge—through the coils that are kept cool with ice until it reaches the tap.)

Ken and his group had no shortage of choices for their adventure. Sierra Nevada, which built its name upon its pale ale (still the brewer's best seller), now widely distributes thirty-five beers over the course of the year, with many more available at the breweries in Chico and Mills River, North Carolina, and the Sierra Nevada tasting room in Berkeley. In addition to its many wonderful beers, Ken and his team have set a high standard for responsible business practices; the Chico brewery has earned national recognition for its minimal environmental impact.

There are many fine spots along the Middle Fork to enjoy a pint. A high point for Ken came toward the end of his float. "There were some hot springs along the bank, a little upstream of one of our last camps," he recalled. "We grabbed one of the kegs and some ice, packed it in a plastic garbage bag, and hauled it up to the springs. We eased our way in, filled up our glasses, and toasted our good fortune."

KEN GROSSMAN is the founder, president, and CEO of Sierra Nevada Brewing Company. Ken has a long history of community service and a strong interest in the environment. As owner of a large property on Big Chico Creek that includes the principal holding pool for Chinook salmon, Ken is dedicated to the stewardship of river ecosystems. He is a trustee of River Partners and a strong supporter of numerous environmental groups. Ken studied chemistry and physics at Butte College and California State University, Chico.

If You Go

▶ **Getting There:** Most rafters fly into Boise; from there it's a three-hour drive to Stanley or a short flight. McCall Aviation (800-992-6559; www.mccallaviation.com) provides air-taxi service to Stanley and Salmon (near the take-out).

▶ **Best Time to Visit:** Most float the Middle Fork from June through September; water can be high and fast in the early spring, and a little "skinny" in late summer. A number of outfitters lead trips on the Middle Fork, including Solitude River Trips (208-806-1218; www.rivertrips.com).

▶ **Spots to Visit:** Redfish Lake Lodge (208-774-3536; www.redfishlake.com) sits on beautiful Redfish Lake and has several local beers on tap for the night before your trip launches.

▶ **Accommodations:** Mountain Village Lodge (800-843-5475; www.mountainvillage.com) is recommended for lodging in Stanley before trips launch.

DESTINATION **22**

CHICAGO

RECOMMENDED BY **Elizabeth Garibay**

"If you get into a conversation with any Chicagoan, they're going to tell you pretty quickly that they're from Chicago," Liz Garibay ventured. "They are, by and large, fiercely loyal, hard-working, blue-collar folks from an immigrant background. Really good people. You walk down the street looking lost, someone will try to help you. It's that kind of place. When I'd go into a bar in some cities and try to strike up a conversation, most people were not very friendly. It was as though they thought I wanted something from them. That's not the case in Chicago. Walk into most bars here, you'll make friends."

Chicago—the Windy City, the City of Big Shoulders, Chi-Town—is also the City by the Lake. For Liz, the source of the city's thriving beer culture can be traced to its proximity to Lake Michigan and the presence of many immigrants of German descent. "During Prohibition, the lake was a great conduit for bringing beer (and other spirits) into town," Liz explained. "When people think of Chicago history, they think of the railroads, the stockyards. They may not realize the impact early German settlers had. In the early days, it really was a German town. The immigrants brought certain skill sets from home that shaped the city—butchery, baking, brewing. In the 1850s, there were many breweries popping up, and by 1870, the brewing business was booming. If it weren't for the beer industry, we might not be here! The fire [of 1871] destroyed everything, including the breweries. Some of the bigger brewers moved north to Milwaukee; the smaller ones were able to get back on their feet faster. When people talk about the craft beer revolution here, I think of more of the craft beer evolution. We keep repeating what happened."

Most would agree that a bellwether in Chicago's recent evolutionary phase was the opening of Goose Island in 1988. "John Hall, the founder, spent time traveling in Europe," Liz explained. "When he was in England, he fell in love with English ales. Soon

OPPOSITE:
Most agree that
Chicago's brewing
renaissance began
with John Hall
and the opening
of Goose Island.

after he read of the burgeoning beer scene in Northern California. It inspired him to start a brewery." Today, Goose Island brews 24/7 from a fifty-barrel facility, with more than fifty bottled ales (including a number of bourbon-aged brews) and two brewpubs to its credit. "There are seventy breweries in the Chicagoland region," Liz added. "They run the gamut from Half Acre, which specializes in hop-forward styles, to 5 Rabbit Cerveceria, a Latino-owned brewery that infuses Latin American culture into its products—like a passion fruit wheat beer. Almost all of the breweries have six or less degrees of separation from Goose Island."

When asked to lead a virtual tour of her favorite Chicago beer bars, it's no surprise that Liz's stops reflect the city's rich tavern history. "Old Town is a favorite neighborhood for me. It was the original settlement area for Germans. Today, it's an idyllic oasis in the middle of the city, and a favorite haunt there is Twin Anchors. The building dates back to the 1880s, and there was a tavern operating on the spot in 1910. People love to talk about how their bar was a speakeasy, but it's usually hard to prove. Twin Anchors was a well-documented speakeasy. The guy who ran the speakeasy was also a harbormaster at Monroe Harbor and had access to Canada via the lake. He and his business partner both had a love of the sea, and after Prohibition, they named it Twin Anchors. There's a main bar and a restaurant that's gained a reputation for its ribs. In the fifties, Frank Sinatra would often go here when he was in town. He had his own booth and even had a phone installed. For me, it's the quintessential Chicago corner tap.

"A five-minute walk away is the Old Town Ale House. It's right across the street from Second City [Chicago's famous comedy club] and has connections to Chicago's folk-music scene. (Old Town was the Chicago equivalent to Haight-Ashbury—our counterculture.) Old Town's music history lives on the jukebox. Overall, you feel transported to another time there. The people that once owned the tavern gave the bar to its workers. On the walls, there are a host of portraits painted by one of the current owners, Bruce Elliott. There had been an original mural of regulars, and Bruce started painting pictures of more-current regulars and Second City personalities like Bill Murray and Dan Aykroyd. Bruce is politically active, and he started painting more-controversial images—like a naked Sarah Palin, on a polar bear rug clutching an assault rifle.

"There are so many different neighborhoods in Chicago, so many hidden treasures as far as bars are concerned. The neighborhoods are very walkable. I suggest avoiding downtown and getting on a train. Get off somewhere that looks interesting and explore.

Wherever you're staying, you can find a brewery or craft beer bar. Chicago is becoming the best beer city you've never heard of."

ELIZABETH GARIBAY created History on Tap in 2002—a project that explores Chicago's past through its great saloons—to combine her love for pubs, history, and her native city. Her writing, History Pub Crawls (for the Chicago History Museum), and other endeavors have been lauded by the *Huffington Post*, the *Los Angeles Times*, the *Chicago Tribune*, *Time Out*, the *Toronto Star*, the *Scotsman*, the *Berliner Kurier*, an assortment of other media and cultural organizations, and an array of happy tavern and brewery owners. Liz's iPhone/Android app, Chicago Taverns & Tales, has been called one of the best Chicago apps available. She is the only American to have ever been invited to join the prestigious and boozy organization known as the Pub History Society of the United Kingdom. When she's not off giving tours or talks, consulting for museums and breweries, writing for global publications, or discovering new tales, taverns, and towns, Liz is probably tucked away in one of her favorite ale houses, root, root, rooting for her beloved Chicago Cubs. She also serves on the board of directors of the Eastland Disaster Historical Society and on the steering committee of the LGBT Community Fund of the Chicago Community Trust.

If You Go

▶ **Getting There:** Chicago is served by most carriers.
▶ **Best Time to Visit:** Chicago Craft Beer Week is held in mid-May each year.
▶ **Spots to Visit:** Goose Island (800-466-7363; www.gooseisland.com); Twin Anchors (312-266-1616; www.twinanchorsribs.com); the Old Town Ale House (312-944-7020; www.theoldtownalehouse.com).
▶ **Accommodations:** Choose Chicago (www.choosechicago.com) lists lodging options around the Windy City.

23

DESTINATION

NIHIWATU

RECOMMENDED BY **Terry Simms**

As a renowned surfing instructor, Terry Simms travels to some of the world's most beautiful beaches. But after a while, even the most beautiful beaches can begin to look a bit the same. "Sometimes, the beer that's served helps ground me, helps jog my memory," Terry mused. "If it's Dos Equis, I know I'm in Mexico. If it's Imperial, I'm in Costa Rica. And if it's Bintang, I'm on the island of Sumba in Indonesia, at Nihiwatu."

Though Indonesia is a Muslim majority country, alcohol is tolerated in most regions—perhaps a nod to the nation's secularist leanings. Before the arrival of the Dutch, those beverages took the form of palm wine and various derivatives. Beer arrived with the colonialists in the nineteenth century. Many visitors will note the similarity between Bir Bintang and Heineken, and with good reason. The first Heineken brewery was established in the East Indies in 1929. The brewery was appropriated by Indonesia in the 1950s after the country gained independence; in the sixties Heineken resumed operations, under the name Bintang. Today, this easy-drinking pilsner is by far Indonesia's most popular beer, and one of the country's best-known consumer brands. (In a nod to Heineken, the Bintang label shares the Dutch brand's red star.)

Terry was initially drawn to Nihiwatu by rumors of the proverbial perfect wave, which surf-industry insiders have dubbed "God's Left." He's been drawn back again and again—often with students in tow—by the vibe of the place. "I believe that there are certain power points around the world that give off a positive energy," Terry continued. "I've surfed all over the world, and Nihiwatu exudes some of the most powerful natural spirituality that I've experienced anywhere. Nihiwatu is actually the name for a sacrificial rock on one edge of the beach. This beach is not just a place where the people harvest seaweed and octopus off the reef and wash their buffalo. It's a sacred place of worship."

OPPOSITE: A rider takes on the break at Nihiwatu, which has been dubbed "God's Left."

Sumba rests midway between better-known Bali and East Timor and has retained much of its original character. Interlopers from Europe and beyond were discouraged from colonization by the fierce reputation of Sumba's headhunting warriors. (Headhunting was *officially* outlawed in the 1950s, though incidences occurred into the 1990s; the good news is that enmities tend to be directed against opposing clans.) When the Dutch did establish a garrison on the northeastern end of the island in the late nineteenth century, their control barely extended beyond its walls. Claude and Petra Graves arrived in 1988, seeking a place for a special kind of eco-resort, and Sumba met all their criteria—seclusion, pristine beaches, thriving indigenous cultures—and in the case of Nihiwatu, a mind-blowing break. After overcoming many impasses in the course of a dozen years, including a territorial dispute with local tribes and an earthquake that destroyed the first iteration of the resort—Nihiwatu emerged. The 438-acre property wraps along a mile and a half of private beach, guarded on each end by headlands.

The magic of the place is apparent from the moment you arrive. "From the tiny airstrip where you land on Sumba, it's about two hours through the jungle to the entrance to Nihiwatu," Simms continued. "You come up over a hill, and there's the beach. The stunning thing is, there's no one there. No one fishing, no one walking on the beach. The lodge and bungalows are so well integrated into the topography that all you see upon arrival is the perfect wave and the Horizon Pool above the lodge. Most guests are pretty tired upon arrival, especially if you flew into Bali (point of departure for Sumba) on the previous day. But the water is so blue and the sand so white, you get a burst of energy. On one of my first visits to Nihiwatu, I was walking along the beach with my board, when suddenly a group of water buffalo came thundering out of the jungle. There were little naked boys—six or eight years old—herding the buffalo toward the surf. I was startled and even a little scared at first, and then I realized that the kids had brought the buffalo to the surf so they could wash off after plowing the fields. This definitely wasn't Maui!"

The nuances of waves—beyond being big or small—are lost on most non-surfers. Terry succinctly explained the advantages of Nihiwatu's break. "Most world-class waves are reliable to produce one size or type of wave, or to be at their best for a very limited period of time. The beauty of the left break at Nihiwatu is that it starts breaking at one foot and goes all the way to twenty feet in size. It breaks consistently all year, the winds are complimentary, and thanks to lodge rules, there are never more than nine surfers on the beach. This is perfect for teaching, as there are never crowds, and there's a wide range of wave sizes to accommodate first-day surfers and experts alike. To me, surfing is about two things—safety and releasing your inner spirit. I try to give people a chance to experience an extreme activity without an extreme risk, to have the joy and fun they may not have had since childhood. I've taught twelve-month-old babies and senior citizens. Age, weight, athleticism have nothing to do with it; if you have the desire, you can surf."

There are few better ways to cap off a fine day of wave riding than with a cold beer. For Terry, there's no better place to enjoy a Bintang than the bar at Nihiwatu. "You're on a twenty-foot bluff, with tropical forest all around you," he described. "To the right, there's a white-sand beach reflecting the golden light of the sunset. The surf comes in right below the bar, the thud of it hitting the beach echoing up. It reverberates, sometimes coinciding with the music that's playing on the stereo.

"A beer at that bar on that island is transcendental."

TERRY "SIMBA" SIMMS started surfing at age seven, gave his first surfing lesson at age ten, and has been traveling and teaching surfing ever since. A former longboard champion, Simms was on the professional circuit for ten years and has been frequently featured in the surfing press. He helped create Shared Adventures, a nonprofit company that takes the physically challenged for free surfing, diving, whale watching, kayaking and sailing outings. Through his travels and teaching, Simms strives to help people and the ocean come together.

If You Go

▶ **Getting There:** The island of Sumba is reached via Bali; you'll need to overnight near the airport in Denpasar to catch the morning flight to Sumba the next day.
▶ **Best Time to Visit:** March and April see more modest waves, best for beginners; May to September sees larger waves.
▶ **Spots to Visit:** Nihiwatu (+62 361 757 149; www.nihiwatu.com) accepts just twenty-five visitors at a time, only nine of which can surf. Terry Simms leads several surf instruction trips to Nihiwatu each year. Contact him about availability at simbasurf@yahoo.com.

DESTINATION 24

RIVER MOY

RECOMMENDED BY **Kirk Deeter**

"Ireland is known for its salmon fishing and for its pubs," Kirk Deeter began. "I don't think I've ever experienced a closer connection between fly-fishing lore—past and present—and pub culture than V.J. Doherty's Ridge Pool Bar, on the banks of Ireland's most famous salmon river, the Moy."

The River Moy rises in the Ox Mountains of County Sligo in northwest Ireland and flows sixty-two miles before entering the Atlantic at Killala Bay, County Mayo. Its perpetually tea-colored waters—thanks to the presence of peat deposits along much of its course—host impressive numbers of returning Atlantic salmon each spring and summer. On a good year, fisheries managers estimate that seventy-five thousand salmon return to the Moy, making it Ireland's most prolific salmon river. Atlantic salmon have long had a strong pull for anglers, in part for their beauty and fine table presentation; in part for their proclivity for long, leaping battles; and in part for their inscrutable ways. Sometimes they will take a fly, sometimes they won't; this unpredictable behavior has a perverse appeal for fly fishers who like a challenge . . . though the number of fish in the Moy improves one's odds. (Atlantic salmon on some rivers can reach over fifty pounds; on the Moy, fish average closer to eight pounds.)

Most Atlantic salmon rivers—be they in northern Norway, Iceland, or Labrador—are situated far from population centers, often in wilderness areas, as such environs provide the cold, clean water these fish need to thrive. The River Moy is an exception to this rule; the river's most fecund stretches rest smack in the middle of town. Anglers here are more likely to have their concentration disrupted by the beeping horns of a wedding party than the splashing of a moose or bear crossing the river behind them. Unlike fishing at your local lake or stream, one cannot merely show up on the banks of a salmon river like the

OPPOSITE:
If the Atlantic salmon aren't cooperative, solace in the shape of a Guinness awaits at V.J. Doherty's Ridge Pool Bar (just beyond the bridge).

DESTINATION

25

115

Moy and begin casting. Instead, you must lease a "beat," which entitles you to fish a section of river for a predetermined amount of time for a fee. The cost of a beat depends on its reputation for producing fish. On the River Moy, no beat is more sought after than the Ridge Pool, smack in the middle of town. Instead of granitic canyons or deep boreal forests, the right bank of the Moy backs up to a stone wall, above which is Ridge Pool Road, with assorted storefronts (including two tackle shops) and a promenade where passersby may pause to critique your casting from sidewalks. The left bank is skirted by a neatly cobbled sidewalk, the office of Inland Fisheries Ireland (where local gillies—fishing guides—might grab a cup of coffee as they assess your tackle), the Ballina Manor Hotel, and finally, V.J. Doherty's . . . which many anglers would consider a perfect procession.

"There's an orderly logic to how anglers fish the Ridge Pool," Kirk continued. "The first angler steps in at the top (most upstream) section of the pool and begins casting. Once his line is out, he takes two steps downstream after each cast. After he's proceeded forty yards downstream, another angler enters at the top of the pool. When the first two anglers have proceeded forty yards downstream, another angler enters the pool. There are no more than five or six anglers in the beat during a given session. Once the first angler has reached the bottom of the pool, he leaves the water. From here, there are several options: Return to the top of the beat for another fishing session; stop at Inland Fisheries Office for a cup of coffee; or walk up the steps to V.J. Doherty's. Its location makes it a perfect pit stop before returning to the top of the beat. You don't have to stop . . . but you should."

V.J. Doherty's Ridge Pool Bar was established in 1913 by its namesake; it remains in the family today, currently operated by the founder's great-grandson. The dark polished bar and soft lighting give the pub a warm glow, a pleasing contrast to the drizzle that often accompanies a session on the river. The walls are festooned with fly-fishing memorabilia, photos of anglers with their catch, antique rods, and shadow boxes containing renowned Moy fly patterns with whimsical names like the Hairy Mary, Thunder and Lightning, and Blue Charm. "At the Ridge Pool Bar, you can wear your waders inside," Kirk added, "and you're not the only one in waders. The bartender will give you a garbage bag to place over the barstool as he's slowly pouring your Guinness."

You can walk into a pub in Ireland and order a Murphy's or a Beamish and have a perfectly satisfactory stout experience. But the majority of pub visitors (tourists and locals alike) are more likely to request a Guinness. The dark draught (not black, aficionados will assure you, but a very deep shade of ruby) was created by Arthur Guinness in 1759 in Dublin; stout is still brewed at the original St. James's Gate site today. Guinness's deep color comes from roasting a portion of the barley; the creamy head from mixing nitrogen with the ale as it's poured. (The precise recipe is not known.) Though celebrated as a "meal in a mug" by its proponents, Guinness is less caloric that you might think (roughly two hundred calories in a twenty-ounce imperial pint) and also less potent, with an ABV of 4.2 percent . . . which is to say, weaker than a Budweiser, which comes in at 5 percent. The pouring of a Guinness is nearly as much a ritual as the drinking of a Guinness. While some American bartenders may attempt to accelerate the process, the publicans at the Ridge Pool Bar understand that the goodness of Guinness cannot be rushed. Fergal Murray, Guinness's master brewer, has provided some guidelines for the perfect pour:

1. Hold the glass at a 45-degree angle and fill the glass to three-quarters full.
2. Place the glass on a flat surface and allow the stout to settle for 119.5 seconds
3. When time has elapsed, put the glass back under the tap and fill until the head is just above the rim of the pint glass. The head should be ¾" to 1" high.

"When you lease a beat on the Ridge Pool, you have access to the river for six hours. It takes about one and a half hours to fish the pool from top to bottom. During my fishing session, I stopped at V.J. Doherty's after each pass through before returning to my place in the queue of anglers working the beat. On the first two visits, you can revisit your fishing strategies and make a new battle plan. The Guinness is mild enough that your thoughts don't get muddled. After the third pass through the pool, you're either assuaging your frustrations or celebrating your catch. Either way, a stop at the Ridge Pool Bar is a victory."

KIRK DEETER is media director at Trout Unlimited, where his responsibilities include editing *Trout* magazine. He is also an editor at large for *Field & Stream* magazine and the editor in chief of *Angling Trade*. His stories have appeared in *Garden & Gun*, the *Drake*, *5280*, *Fly Rod & Reel*, *Fly Fisherman*, *Big Sky Journal*, *Salt Water Sportsman*, and *Trout*, among other places. Kirk is also the coauthor of four books: *The Orvis Guide to Fly Fishing for Carp*, *The Little Red Book of Fly Fishing* (with Charlie Meyers), *Castworks: Reflections of Fly Fishing Guides and the American West* (Game & Fish Mastery Library; with Andrew W.

DESTINATION

25

Steketee and Liz Steketee), and *Tideline: Captains, Fly-Fishing and the American Coast* (with Andrew W. Steketee and Marco Lorenzetti).

If You Go

▶ **Getting There:** The airport most convenient to County Mayo is in Knock, which is served from Dublin by Aer Arann (www.aerarann.com) and London by Ryanair (www. ryanair.com).

▶ **Best Time to Visit:** The Atlantic salmon season is open from February through September, though the best fishing is generally in July and August.

▶ **Spots to Visit:** V.J. Doherty's Ridge Pool Bar. A host of other pubs are within a short walk.

▶ **Accommodations:** Mount Falcon Estate (+353 96 74472; www.mountfalcon.com) is just a few miles up the road from downtown Ballina and caters to anglers and golfers . . . and serves a fine Guinness too.

DUBLIN

RECOMMENDED BY **Colm Quilligan**

Writers and alcohol have often walked—perhaps stumbled—uneasily together through modern literary history. Baudelaire and Rimbaud dabbled in absinthe. Faulkner was fueled by bourbon, often in the vehicle of a mint julep. Hemingway, if his first-person narrators are any indication, could find solace in just about any spirited beverage.

Given its modest population, Ireland has enjoyed an outsize literary output, especially in the first half of the twentieth century. And Irish literary tradition has always been linked closely to the pub culture of Dublin. There's little doubt that the cryptic dialogue of Samuel Beckett and the bon mots of Oscar Wilde were not occasionally inspired by the odd pint of Guinness. But pubs also served a more practical purpose for Irish writers of a certain time, as Colm Quilligan explained.

"It was commonplace for Dublin writers to meet editors and publishers in pubs to try to interest them in their work. This was especially true between 1930 and 1960, when the writing of so many authors was being banned. Writers could feel freer to express themselves in the convivial atmosphere of the pub. There was also the opportunity to network. The Irish are the greatest talkers the world has had since the Greeks, and the pubs provided a gregarious, almost conspiratorial atmosphere for them to talk and make connections, away from official Ireland. If you happened to have a story published in the *Irish Times*, you might be paid five pounds—a lot of money back then. Sometimes you would get paid in the pub, and your friends would help you spend it."

The roots of Dublin's pub culture date back over eight hundred years; the Brazen Head, Ireland's oldest pub, opened its doors in 1198. While whiskey was the drink of choice in the countryside, historian Kevin Kearns notes that ale was the common beverage in Dublin by the twelfth century, with most brewed by women in their homes. It's

surmised that homes that brewed ale with a good reputation evolved into public houses as customers began to linger to consume the ale they'd purchased. By the seventeenth century, Dublin had perhaps become a bit too enchanted with its ale houses; records show that for a city with roughly 4,000 families, there were 1,180 taverns. Visitors to Dublin were taken aback by its number of drinking establishments and the general insobriety of its citizenry. (One account from the time even suggested that the crypt in Christ Church Cathedral had been converted into a tavern.) When Arthur Guinness arrived in Dublin in 1759 and signed a nine-thousand-year lease for a four-acre property at St. James's Gate, the city was assured an even more stable flow of ale . . . an ale that would take on a darker shade. (The lease that Guinness had drawn up is on display at the brewery.)

OPPOSITE:
The Brazen Head is Ireland's oldest pub, dating back to 1198.

There's considerable debate about the origin of stout, though there's little argument that Guinness has made the beer category its own—at least in part by its memorable advertising campaigns, which in the 1930s and 1940s featured whimsical drawings by John Gilroy of toucans, seals, and kangaroos. Even the most occasional beer drinker may recall some of the more famous slogans—"Guinness for Strength," "Lovely Day for a Guinness," and "Guinness Is Good for You." According to the company, 1.8 billion pints are sold around the world each year. No trip to Dublin—whether you're a beer drinker or not—is quite complete without a sojourn to St. James's Gate.

Though Guinness certainly flows freely in many Dublin pubs, stout is no longer the only game in town. Scores of craft breweries have opened in the last decade, along with pubs emphasizing a greater variety of beer styles. One such pub, Against the Grain, made the bold decision to not offer Guinness when it opened in 2010. Many believed it would not see 2011, but as of this writing, it's going strong.

Colm has been drawn to the pubs of Dublin less by their taps and more by their literary lore. "It always seemed to me that in Dublin, the pub, the poet, and the pint were inseparable," he continued. "When we started the Dublin Literary Pub Crawl in 1988, the idea was to get the words of our great writers off the page and onto the street." Working with Frank Smith, Colm leads guests to several pubs frequented by Dublin's past literati, sharing snippets of history, reeling off quotes from James Joyce's *Ulysses*, and even performing a scene from Samuel Beckett's existential drama *Waiting for Godot*. Colm described a few of his favorite stops along the way.

"Though many of the great pubs from when *Ulysses* takes place [1904] have closed down, half a dozen are still going strong. Davy Byrnes may be the best known. It figures

DESTINATION

26

in the Lestrygonians chapter. Bloom goes into another pub called Burton's to get lunch but is disgusted by the meat smell. He leaves and heads to Davy Byrnes and orders a gorgonzola sandwich and a glass of burgundy. You can place a similar order today, and it would set you back €12.95. Across the street is the Bailey, which was very popular in the postwar generation. Charlie Chaplin was a frequent visitor to the Bailey, as was the poet and novelist Patrick Kavanagh; Seamus Heaney came here in 1965 to meet Kavanagh. The Palace Bar on Fleet Street is right across the street from the building that houses the *Irish Times* and was an important literary meeting spot, with gatherings led by Robert M. Smyllie, editor of the *Times*. Right around the corner, there's McDaids Pub. This was the unofficial home of *Envoy* literary magazine, and a haunt of Brendan Behan, who famously described himself as a drinker with writing problems."

When asked about his preferred pint, Colm laughed. "A glass of red wine, actually. I'm not a beer drinker."

COLM QUILLIGAN is owner of Dublin Literary Pub Crawl and author of *Dublin Literary Pub Crawl: A Guide to the Literary Pubs of Dublin and the Writers They Served*, which was published in 2008.

If You Go

▶ **Getting There:** Dublin is served by many major carriers, including Aer Lingus (800-474-7424; https://new.aerlingus.com).

▶ **Best Time to Visit:** Joyce devotees will want to visit in mid-June to celebrate Bloomsday, June 16. Literary pub crawls (+353 1 6705602; www.dublinpubcrawl.com) are offered throughout the year.

▶ **Spots to Visit:** The Brazen Head (+353 1 677 9549; www.brazenhead.com); Guinness Storehouse (+353 1 408 4800; www.guinness-storehouse.com); Davy Byrnes (+353 1 677 5217; www.davybyrnes.com); the Bailey (+353 1 670 4939; www.baileybarcafe.com); the Palace Bar (+353 1 671 7388; www.thepalacebardublin); McDaids (+353 1 679 4395).

▶ **Accommodations:** Visit Dublin (www.visitdublin.com) lists a range of lodging options around the city.

NORTHERN ITALY

RECOMMENDED BY **Mike Saxton**

It's a gastronomic fantasy come true: a foodie journey through the Piedmont. Plates of *salame* and *insalata di carne cruda* arrived accompanied by *grissini*, the ubiquitous bread-sticks of Turin. Bowls of gnocchi sprinkled with Grana Padano are joined by *brasato al Barolo*, featuring prime cuts from celebrated Piemontese cattle. All of these wonderful delicacies are washed down with a shimmering golden ale.

Ale?

It's enough to make your dear departed Nonni roll over in her grave!

Beer is not about to displace Barberas and Moscatos from the tables of Northern Italy, but it's earning true legitimacy. The number of commercial brewers in Italy has grown from fewer than ten in the mid-1990s to over six hundred, with the greatest concentration in the northern regions of Piedmont and Lombardy. Americans who might equate Italian beer with Peroni or Moretti—both rather unremarkable lagers—will be taken aback by the inventive recipes many brewers are unveiling. Not tethered to a long and storied brewing tradition, the Italians feel free to use those ingredients that are available, be it roses, black currant, licorice, juniper, or chestnuts.

Mike Saxton recalls when his eyes were opened to the grain possibilities of northern Italy. "I was at Cantillon Brewery in Brussels back in 2008 for one of their open brew days. I met some Italian brewers there, and we opened some of the bottles they'd brought along. My thinking at the time was, 'Wow, you're making this in Italy? I need to begin looking into this.' I soon learned that B. United International was importing some Italian craft beers into the United States. I also came upon an Italian website (www.micro birrifici.org) that listed every microbrewery and brewpub in Italy. I did a good deal of research to come up with a list of the most-interesting beer stops in the north, and made my first trip in 2009. It went so well, I've led several trips back since."

The Italian beer tour that Mike has assembled begins in Monterosso al Mare (part of Cinque Terre) and wanders east and north in a generally clockwise direction before ending in Milan. The itinerary certainly stresses the eclectic—and at times downright eccentric—brews of the Piedmont and Lombardy regions, but there's also an opportunity to get a taste of northern Italy's other appeals. After flying into Milan, guests generally take a train to Monterosso al Mare. There's a day to explore the five marvelously terraced villages (Vernazza, Corniglia, Manarola, and Riomaggiore, in addition to Monterosso al Mare) that hang above the Ligurian coast before departing for Genoa and a private beer tasting at La Fabbrica di Birra Busalla, complete with local salami and focaccia. Dinner that evening is at Locanda del Grue, where a special late-summer beer menu awaits, featuring the award-winning creations of master brewer Riccardo Franzosi of Birrificio di Montegioco. (Franzosi will join the group if possible.) Many of Montegioco's beers are barrel aged, in keeping with the maturation process used by the area's wine makers. A few of their more notable products include Quarta Runa, made with local Volpedo peaches, and Tibir, which includes Timorasso grapes.

After a detour along the coast to the south to visit the olive oil museum in the town of Imperia and a beer lunch in Diano Marina with Manuel Giacometti of Birrificio Chevalier, your Italian birra tour de force moves north to Vernante, at the edge of the Maritime Alps. "Vernante was the home of Attilio Mussino, the illustrator of Pinocchio," Mike continued, "and there are murals all over town based on his paintings. One of my favorite stops is here, Birrificio Troll. It's located up a valley amidst a birch forest in the mountains. They have a seasonal beer called Palanfrina that's brewed in the fall and made with local chestnuts. It's strong (9 percent ABV), but the chestnuts make for a nutty, slightly sweet flavor. On my first trip to Italy I tried to arrange a visit, but the brewer, Alberto, didn't get back to me. We were at our hotel in Vernante, and I asked the manager about Troll. It turned out that Alberto was down in the basement of the hotel tasting wine. The manager called down and said there were some Americans who wanted to see the brewery. I don't speak Italian and Alberto can't speak English, but we both speak French. After a brief conversation, he declared that he would open up the brewery just for our group and grill some sausages to go with the beer."

There are a few more stops as you wind north before reaching Milan, including a visit to Fontanafredda, to sample some fine Piemontese Barberas (you are in Italy, after all).

One of the most memorable is in the village of Piozzo for dinner at Birreria Le Baladin, Teo Musso's brewery. Musso launched Baladin in 1996 and is widely credited with putting Italy on the craft beer map. Though he grew up in a wine-drinking family, Musso had an early interest in beer—an interest that became an avocation after tasting a bottle of Chimay Blue Cap. After running a creperie named Le Baladin, Teo spent a stint tasting and brewing in Belgium. When he returned to Piozzo this time, Le Baladin the brewpub was born. Now, he boasts fifteen locations as far afield as New York. During dinner at Birreria Le Baladin, you'll have the opportunity to sample some of the more than thirty flavors, which range from Nora (based on a ninth-century Egyptian recipe using unmalted kamut to Super Baladin (a Belgian tripel that employs English yeast in the first fermentation and Belgian yeast in a second bottle fermentation).

MIKE SAXTON is the founder and owner of Beer Trips (www.beertrips.com), which has led beer-inspired journeys around the world since 1998.

If You Go

▶ **Getting There:** The trip described above begins and ends in Milan, which is served by most major international carriers. Most guests will take the train from Milan to Monterosso; reservations can be made at www.trenitalia.com.

▶ **Best Time to Visit:** Beer Trips generally plans its Northern Italy trips for late summer/ early fall.

▶ **Spots to Visit:** A few of the highlights from the adventure described above include Birra Troll (+39 0171-920143; www.birratroll.it) and Birreria Le Baladin (+39 0173-795431; www.baladin.it). Beer Trips (406-531-9109; www.beertrips.com) can greatly facilitate your trip (including transportation, hotel accommodation and private tours/dinners with leading brewers).

▶ **Accommodations:** A few of the hotels that Mike recommends include Albergo Nazionale (+39 0171-920181) in Vernante; Hotel Savona (+39 0173-440440; www.hotel savona.com) in Alba; and Starhotels Anderson (+39 02 6690141; www.starhotels.com) in Milan. A comprehensive list of lodging options resides at www.italia.it.

PORTLAND

RECOMMENDED BY **Kathleen Pierce**

Portland—the picturesque and diminutive city (population around seventy thousand) that rests two hours north of Boston along Maine's Casco Bay—has emerged as one of America's foodie hotspots. Some nights it can be difficult to navigate the cobblestoned streets of the Old Port neighborhood, given the unfurling cables of Food Channel film crews and klieg lights accompanying *Bon Appétit* photo shoots. Be it french fries cooked in duck fat or the latest creation from a passel of James Beard Award–winning chefs, Portland has arrived.

Put another way: It's not just for lobster rolls anymore.

The food craze that has enveloped Maine's largest city has also served to elevate its contributions to the brewing arts. "All the attention to food in Portland has extended to the beer offerings—and the two together," Kathleen Pierce opined. "Many of the restaurateurs are going out of their way to make sure they have a great beer selection. I think that's how some of the restaurants are surviving—people are coming in looking for local beers."

The dawn of modern craft brewing in Portland can be traced to late 1986, when David Geary and his wife, Karen, poured the first pints of Geary's Pale Ale. Geary had become curious about craft beer while traveling in Scotland a few years earlier and befriending the Twentieth Laird of Traquair, Peter Maxwell Stewart. Stewart happened to keep a small brewery in his castle (below the chapel, where it had initially been in the early 1700s), and was happy to share his brewing insights with Geary. With Stewart's help, Geary visited (and worked) at a number of commercial breweries in the United Kingdom before returning to Portland intent on starting his own establishment. He was turned down for funding more than one hundred times before he realized his dream. The D.L. Geary Brewing

OPPOSITE:
Little Tap House
rests just above
Portland's
Old Port
neighborhood
and is helping
make the
picturesque
coastal city
a beer
destination.

DESTINATION

28

Company is still going strong, brewing a dozen beers and distributing their wares to fifteen states. Geary was followed a few years later by Shipyard (in 1994), which has grown to be one of America's larger craft breweries, shipping their signature Export Ale to all fifty states, and Allagash Brewing, which began selling beer in 1995 and has built a national reputation with its Belgian-inspired ales, particularly Allagash White. As of this writing, Portland boasts a dozen small breweries, with a smattering of other operations to the north and south.

"One trend I've seen recently is that many of the breweries are expanding their tasting rooms, and people are meeting in tasting rooms for a few beers instead of a bar," explained Kathleen. "Some late afternoons and evenings, you'll have food trucks showing up to support the model. It's a whole scene. Allagash has one, and Geary opened one recently. One I particularly like is Oxbow, which leans toward Belgian-style ales. The original brewer is up the coast a bit in Newcastle, but they opened a facility [Oxbow Blending & Bottling] in the Munjoy Hill neighborhood, on the hillside east of downtown. It has a speakeasy feeling. When you go through the door, you enter into a warehouse that they've turned into a huge space—mostly tasting room, though some of their sour beers are aged there, and they do some bottling. They'll have anywhere from six to a dozen beers on tap. Up the road twenty minutes, in Freeport, there's the Maine Beer Company. They have an excellent tasting room, with all the taps handmade by a local artist." When you're done, you're only a stone's throw from the L.L.Bean retail store, still open twenty-four hours a day, 365 days a year.

In addition to two brewpubs (Gritty McDuff's and Sebago Brewing), Portland boasts a host of fine beer bars. Kathleen weighed in on a few favorites. "The Little Tap House is just up the hill from the waterfront, and they have a ton of Maine beers on tap [fourteen, to be exact]. They've also assembled a menu that pairs well with the beers they're offering. Little Tap House is very popular with the younger crowd, and they even have weekend events for parents with new babies [the BYOB, or Bring Your Own Baby]. Right down on Commercial Street, which fronts the harbor, there's the King's Head. It sounds like an English pub, and is cozy like one, but it's very advanced from a culinary perspective—a true gastropub, with a great horseshoe bar. The King's Head has roughly forty beers on tap and attracts a local crowd. Right nearby is Liquid Riot, which brews its own beer, distills spirits, and has a nice outdoor deck on the wharf with great views." Novare Res Bier Café, also in the Old Port neighborhood, has an extensive tap list, though is somewhat less regionally focused. Great Lost Bear is a bit removed from Old Port but boasts Portland's most extensive tap list, representing over twenty Maine breweries.

The state of Maine has nearly 3,500 miles of shoreline, and while visiting Portland, it would be a shame not to experience a bit of this majestic, rock-ribbed coast from the water. One option is to board one of Portland Schooner's windjammers for a tour of the harbor and Casco Bay; another is to hop a Casco Bay Lines ferry to Peaks Island, just across the harbor. (Should you opt for the latter, consider a stop at the Inn on Peaks Island, which offers Shipyard products on tap, including a cask-conditioned ale brewed on premises.)

There's a certain magic that envelops northern cities in the summertime as residents are drawn outside to the sun. Portland is no different. On a summer night, the Old Port is swinging with live music from pubs resting on pilings over the harbor. One such establishment is the Portland Lobster Company. Your craft beer will be served in a plastic cup as you stand shoulder to shoulder against the railing above the harbor, rubbing elbows with lobstermen and visitors alike. Now is the chance for your lobster roll, served with mayonnaise on the side. Or you can have your lobster like the Mainers—steamed in the shell, with sides of melted butter and lemon.

KATHLEEN PIERCE fell for newspapers at a young age. When her picture was emblazoned on the front page of her hometown daily, she was hooked. Kathleen began as a sales rep for a string of weeklies, but soon realized that the ink-stained wretches in the newsroom were having more fun. After a year as a barista in Manhattan, she returned to Boston armed with an urgent desire to tell the stories of the street. She earned a master's degree in journalism from Northeastern University. With a diverse background reporting on crime, schools, and the ins and outs of small-town shenanigans for papers across New England, Kathleen went on to become a lifestyle editor and food blogger for the *Lowell Sun*. A former regular contributor to the *Boston Globe*, she moved to Maine in the spring of 2013 to join the *Bangor Daily News*. Based in Greater Portland, Kathleen unearths dynamic stories that straddle culture, business, people, and trends.

DESTINATION

28

If You Go

▶ **Getting There:** Portland is served by many carriers, including Delta (800-221-1212; www.delta.com) and United Airlines (800-864-8331; www.united.com).

▶ **Best Time to Visit:** You can count on fairly good weather between mid-May and mid-October. The Maine Brewers' Guild Beer Festival is generally held the last Saturday in May; Portland Beer Week is held the first week in November.

▶ **Spots to Visit:** D.L. Geary Brewing (207-878-2337; www.gearybrewing.com); Oxbow Blending & Bottling (207-350-0025; www.oxbowbeer.com); Maine Beer Company (207-221-5711; www.mainebeercompany.com); Little Tap House (207-518-9283; www.littletaphouse.com); the King's Head (207-805-1252; www.thekingsheadportland.com); Novare Res Bier Café (207-761-2437; www.novareresbiercafe.com); Great Lost Bear (207-772-0300; www.greatlostbear.com); Inn on Peak's Island (207-766-5100; www.innonpeaks.com); Portland Lobster Company (207-775-2112; www.portlandlobstercompany.com).

▶ **Accommodations:** Visit Portland (207-772-5800; www.visitportland.com) lists accommodations in the city.

DESTINATION 28

BOSTON BEER COMPANY

RECOMMENDED BY **Jim Koch**

Every sacred place has its inner sanctum, a holiest-of-the-holy place. For pilgrims visiting the Vatican, it might be the Sistine Chapel. For music aficionados trekking to Muscle Shoals, Alabama, it might be the control room at FAME Studios. For Jim Koch, it's the Samuel Adams Barrel Room.

"To me, beer never tastes better than at the brewery where it was born," Jim began. "I don't know why this is so. There's no logical explanation as to why Boston Lager tastes better sitting at the brewery than it does at a bar five miles away, but it does. So I have to say that my favorite place to enjoy a beer is right at the brewery in Boston. And my favorite place within the brewery is in the Barrel Room. This is where we first started aging beer in used spirits barrels back in 1992. There are still some barrels left from that initial batch—twenty-three-year-old Sam Adams Triple Bock—that continue to age quietly. It's beer that's old enough to drink itself!"

As of this writing, there are more than 3,500 breweries operating in the United States and many more preparing to come online. Nearly all of these fall into the independent-brewpub, microbrewery, or regional-brewery category; today, a vast majority of Americans live within ten miles of a local brewery. Given the current brewing climate, it may be difficult for younger craft beer aficionados to appreciate the landscape in 1983, where your request for "a good beer" would at best produce a bottle of Michelob, Löwenbräu, or Heineken. (*BeerAdvocate* cites 1983 as the "low-water mark" for twentieth-century brewing in America, with a total of eighty breweries, and six brewers controlling 92 percent of U.S. beer production.) In 1984, the landscape would slowly begin to morph, thanks in very large part to a management consultant with three Harvard degrees—and an avid home brewer—named Jim Koch, and his Boston Beer Company. Boston Beer

Company was not the first craft brewery to appear in America in the late twentieth century. But its good product—and brilliant marketing efforts—put the idea of micro-breweries on the map.

When Boston Beer Company first began delivering Sam Adams Boston Lager to a handful of bars and restaurants around Boston in April of 1985, the brand had a compelling back story—six generations of brewers in the Koch family, a found lager recipe (technically, a Vienna lager) that belonged to his great-great-grandfather, and Jim's revelation, upon cooking a batch up in his kitchen, that he should return to the family's longstanding business. More importantly, Jim, a veteran of one of the leading consultancies of the day (Boston Consulting Group), understood how to use that backstory to foment a revolution (not unlike his front man, Mr. Adams). The initial goal had been to produce five thousand barrels of beer in five years; by year three, production had skyrocketed to thirty-six thousand barrels per annum. Boston Lager had clearly found a niche, and that niche would grow as Jim took to the airwaves—a friendly pitchman in khakis and a denim button-down shirt, extolling the virtues of better recipes and better ingredients. For a certain generation of beer drinkers, Jim Koch is craft beer . . . a term that didn't even exist when his television commercials began running.

Boston Beer Company was not only an innovator in marketing craft beer. Following on the success of Boston Lager, Jim and his colleagues began producing seasonal beers, ranging from a classic Oktoberfest to Porch Rocker, a Bavarian radler (that combines helles lager with lemons). If all this wasn't enough to rattle American taste buds, Boston Beer Company also helped introduce barrel-aged beers to the larger marketplace.

There was a time not so long ago when aging beer in a wooden barrel was no big deal; in fact, it was the only way you could age beer. Wood could be a fickle master; as it's difficult to clean, wooden casks could diminish the taste and overall quality of beer if it wasn't consumed quickly. (Higher hop rates and higher alcohol content could help offset bacterial growth.) On the positive side, a wood barrel does retain some of the flavor of the previous liquids it's held. Scotch, for example, is often housed in used sherry casks for the subtle flavors the casks convey. Why not beer? Today, many brewers will experiment with aging their ales in casks—often oak, sometimes former bourbon or whiskey barrels—for weeks, months, or even a year. The brews that undergo barrel aging are not for the faint of heart. They are complex and often eclipse 10 percent ABV, almost more a wine or cordial than a beer.

OPPOSITE:
Jim Koch relaxes
in the Samuel
Adams Barrel
Room at Boston
Beer Company,
his favorite
spot within
the brewery.

DESTINATION

29

Since those first batches of Triple Bock (a whopping 17.5 percent ABV) were casked in charred oak whiskey barrels in 1992, Boston Beer Company has gone on to produce a number of barrel-aged beers. On the extreme end are Samuel Adams Utopias, which have ranged from the 1999 Millennium (21 percent ABV, aged in bourbon barrels) to the 10th Anniversary release, which was first aged in bourbon casks (from the award-winning Buffalo Trace Distillery), finished in tawny port casks and vintage ruby port casks from Portugal and rum barrels from Nicaragua . . . and topped out at 29 percent ABV. (The current Barrel Room Collection brews include Samuel Adams American Kriek, Samuel Adams New World, Samuel Adams Stony Brook Red, Samuel Adams Thirteenth Hour, and Samuel Adams Tetravis, all sold in 750-milliter cork-finished bottles.)

"The barrel room in Jamaica Plain is walled off from the rest of the brewery," Jim described, "because there are microorganisms unique to certain barrel-aged beers, and we wouldn't want them touching the others. It's a working part of the brewery, but sometimes we'll hold special events down there. In July of 2014, we had a dinner to celebrate our thirtieth anniversary. I invited some of the beer journalists I've known since the beginning, writers who were present at the creation of the craft beer movement. We set up a table, and a local chef paired each course with some of our longstanding favorites like Boston Lager and Double Bock. It was a really cool way of sharing thirty years of craft brewing with people whose roots go back to when it was an eccentric passion shared by a small number of relative misfits."

JIM KOCH is the founder of the Boston Beer Company and brewer of Samuel Adams. As a sixth-generation brewmaster, beer runs in his blood, but the brewing business was bleak when Jim wanted to start his brewery. So he attended Harvard and earned an undergraduate degree and advanced degrees in business and law, taught adventure skills for Outward Bound, and worked for Boston Consulting Group, counseling corporations while also learning from them. In 1984, Jim decided to pursue his dream. Following family tradition, he brewed his great-great-grandfather's lager recipe. Brewing his first batch in his kitchen, he named the beer Samuel Adams Boston Lager. Unbeknownst to Jim, Samuel Adams Boston Lager would soon become a catalyst of the American craft beer revolution. Jim relentlessly focuses on brewing the best beer, emphasizing that quality and flavor are the only standards worth pursuing. Looking to push the brewing envelope, he pioneered the "extreme beer" movement, challenging drinkers' perception of beer with complex, barrel-aged brews like Samuel Adams Triple Bock and Utopias, a beer of great unprecedented flavor and alcohol content. Drawing upon his struggles to start his business, with little advice and no access to loans, Jim started the Samuel Adams Brewing the American Dream program in 2008 to help food and beverage small-business owners and craft brewers gain access to the capital, mentoring, and networks to succeed. Over the past thirty years, Samuel Adams has become America's largest craft brewery but still only accounts for 1 percent of the beer market. Brewing over fifty distinctive styles of Samuel Adams beers, Jim exudes the same care and passion from when he brewed his first batch of Samuel Adams Boston Lager.

If You Go

▶ **Getting There:** Boston is served by most major carriers. The Samuel Adams Boston brewery is easily reached in the Jamaica Plain neighborhood by taking the T (Orange Line) to the Stony Brook stop.

▶ **Best Time to Visit:** Special events are offered throughout the year. The third Thursday of each month there's an open house celebrating a certain theme, with food and beer to complement that theme. The event is free, but a reservation is required.

▶ **Spots to Visit:** Brewery tours are offered Monday through Saturday at the Samuel Adams Brewery (617-368-5080; www.samueladams.com). Tours do not include a visit to the Barrel Room.

▶ **Accommodations:** The Greater Boston Visitors and Convention Bureau (888-733-2678; www.bostonusa.com) lists lodging options throughout the city.

DESTINATION

29

BAJA CALIFORNIA SUR

RECOMMENDED BY **Jordan Gardenhire**

Baja California is a peninsula that extends 660 miles south from the California border. It's bounded on the east by the Sea of Cortez, which separates the peninsula from the rest of Mexico; to the west is the Pacific. The terrain of Baja is quite mountainous, criss-crossed by four major ranges—Sierra Juárez, Sierra de San Pedro Mártir, Sierra de la Giganta, and Sierra de la Laguna. The mountains serve to divert the little moisture that flows over the peninsula, rendering the region quite arid. While at times stark, Baja is a land of rich contrasts—not only the wet and the dry, but the tremendous colors as well. The juxtaposition of the tropical greens and turquoises of the sea and sky with the ochre of the mountains and the pink and gold sands of the beaches is positively startling.

For Jordan Gardenhire, the aridity of Cabo San Lucas expressed itself at least in part by the paucity of craft beer. "I graduated from the University of Colorado and decided I'd take a year in Mexico, learn to surf and learn Spanish," he began. "I came to Cabo and fell in love with the place, and drank a good deal of Pacifico, which is the beer that's available. While I was in Boulder, I had developed a taste for craft beer. That was definitely missing in Baja. Whenever I had friends that wanted to come down and visit, I begged them to bring some craft beer along. I got to thinking that the timing could be right for a craft brewery in Cabo. I was a homebrewer, and I knew the scene. When I began to explore this possibility, the municipality didn't know what sort of permits to issue. I had to explain the notion of craft beer, even the process. There's very little industry in the southern part of Baja California beyond tourism, so it was a very foreign concept."

As anyone who's been to Mexico (or even a Mexican restaurant) can attest, most of the best-known beers from "south of the border"—Corona, Pacifico, Sol, Tecate, and the like—would not be characterized as adventurous. The template for Mexican beer arrived, oddly enough, from Austria, during the very brief reign of Maximilian I (1864–67), and took the shape of the Vienna lager that the brewers accompanying his group were accustomed to making. Over the years, this slightly darker lager has slowly been lightened and weakened, in part to cut costs, in part to provide a beer in keeping with the warm climate. Like in Vienna itself, the powerful market grip of a few major brewers (Grupo Modelo and Cuauhtémoc Moctezuma) is being slightly loosened, thanks to the revision of laws that once gave the big brewers a level of exclusivity and the acquisition of the aforementioned majors by foreign brewing conglomerates. (The foreign owners have taken a more benign stance toward smaller brewers.) As Mexico's foodie scene has thrived, there's also been a desire to provide more local—and more artisanal—brews. "In 2004, there were just a handful of craft brewers in all of Mexico," Jordan continued. "Now we're up to almost three hundred. A Mexican craft brewers' association was formed in 2015 to advocate for independent brewers."

Starting a brewpub in Cabo took some cojones. First, there was the week-long journey to get the brewhouse south on roads that no one would mistake for the Autobahn. Then there was adapting the product for local tastes. "When we opened our first brewpub in San José, people loved the idea," Jordan recalled. "But then the local people would sample our beer and say, 'Wow! That's bitter!' and make faces. They thought our blonde ale was a little too crazy, and it's pretty light by craft beer standards. Fortunately, we had a number of tourists coming by who had had more exposure to craft beer, and that kept us going. The locals started coming around after we created a few new styles. One was Scorpion Negro, a dark beer that was not too bitter or heavy but had a malty, roasted flavor. Five years ago, our raspberry and blonde cream ales were our most popular offerings. Now it's our Peyote Pale Ale. At forty-five IBUs, it's a more aggressive craft beer . . . at least for Cabo." Baja Brewing now has three locations in Baja Sur—in the art district of San José del Cabo, on the terrace of the popular Cabo Villas Beach Resort and Spa in downtown Cabo San Lucas, and on the Cabo marina.

Cabo is well known for its festive, mañana-oriented atmosphere. This is especially true during the spring-break season. Excitement also builds to a fever pitch when the Bisbee's Black & Blue Tournament, the richest marlin-fishing contest in the world, comes to town in October. The Bisbee's tourney pits anglers against each other—and against the black-and-blue marlin that frequent the rich waters of the Sea of Cortez. Some species can eclipse a thousand pounds; they're extremely powerful, capable of reaching speeds of

DESTINATION

30

over fifty miles per hour; and with their spear-shaped jaws, they're capable of mayhem when brought near the boat. While many professional anglers participate, anyone who shows up with a boat, a heavy-duty fishing rod, and an entrance fee of five thousand dollars can participate. Whether you're in a souped-up Viking powerboat or a smallish skiff, the lure of the Bisbee's is the same: the excitement of competition, the camaraderie of fellow big-game anglers, the thrill of testing wits and muscle against one of the world's great sportfish, and the promise of relatively easy money. After all, each participant has a one-in-two-hundred chance of winning one million dollars or more. And there's also the promise of a cold one at Baja Brewing's marina location.

"For me, the perfect Baja beer would come after a day of paddleboarding or kitesurfing off one of the beaches of the East Cape, a little north and east of Cabo," Jordan said. "I'd go for a Peyote Pale—a beer that's well balanced, with some hop character. Sitting under an umbrella, looking out at the Sea of Cortez—that's as good as it gets."

JORDAN GARDENHIRE started brewing beer in his college apartment in Boulder, Colorado. Later he became an accredited brewer and member of the American Brewers Guild and in 2007 founded the Baja Brewing Company with his father, Charlie. When Jordan's not brewing, he enjoys kiteboarding, surfing, and spearfishing.

DESTINATION
30

If You Go

▶ **Getting There:** Cabo San Lucas airport is served by many major carriers.

▶ **Best Time to Visit:** May/June and October/November allow you to avoid the crowds, though weather is pleasant throughout the winter. To catch the Bisbee's Black & Blue Tournament (714-393-6107; www.bisbees.com), visit in late October.

▶ **Spots to Visit:** Each of Baja Brewing's (www.bajabrewingcompany.com) three locations has its own character. The best views are at the Cabo Villas rooftop cantina.

▶ **Accommodations:** Cabo Villas Beach Resort (866-962-2268; www.cabovillas beachresort.com) offers great views and very close proximity to the Baja Brewery Cantina at Cabo Villas Rooftop. Other lodging options are explored at www.visitloscabos.travel.

TRAVERSE CITY

RECOMMENDED BY **Mike Hall**

Traverse City rests at the bottom of Grand Traverse Bay, along the eastern shores of Lake Michigan. The deep woods and many lakes of the surrounding north country region have made Traverse City a four-season resort, popular with golfers, boaters, bicyclists, cross-country skiers, anglers, and those happy just to sit on the many white sand beaches . . . at least in the summertime. Traverse City has long been known as America's cherry capital, producing over 70 percent of the tart cherries grown in the United States. The region—particularly the Leelanau and Old Mission Peninsulas that jut out from Traverse City into Grand Traverse Bay—have emerged in the last few decades as a significant wine-producing region, creating Riesling, Chardonnay, Pinot Grigio, and Gewürztraminer, as well as ice wines.

Craft beer is now taking its place among the north wood's many bounties. And Mike Hall was in on the ground floor.

"Back in the early nineties, I was a consultant with a company that built breweries all over the world," he began. "I worked on almost fifty brewery openings. In 1995, I was involved with the construction and opening of North Peak Brewing in Traverse City. I also did the design for Mackinaw Brewing, and then worked on Traverse Brewing. Though Traverse Brewing is now out of business, several local brewers can be traced back there. Bill Short of Short's Brewing and John Niedermaier and Russell Springsteen, who started Right Brain (Niedermaier later went on to start Terra Firma) all brewed at Traverse. Tina Schuett was a brewer for Right Brain before she started Rare Bird Brewery. The brewing culture here has also benefited from the support we've received from Michigan State University and Central Michigan University, which both have brewing programs." With the seeds of Mike's early handiwork sown, the Traverse City brewing scene blossomed. As

GINGER IN THE RYE - RANCH ...

KIND ALE - HARVEST ALE, WET HOPPED, W/ CASCADE & CHINOOK HOPS ...

SOFT PARADE - RYE ALE FERMENTED W/ LOADS OF STRAWBERRIES, BLUEBERRIES, BLACKBERRIES & RASPBERRIES

KUSAC - SEMI-DRY CIDER W/ SWEET FRUIT & WHITE WINE-LIKE AROMAS

OVERROCK - SEMI-SWEET CIDER W/ DELICATE FRUIT & YEAST AROMAS

HELLACIOUS ROCK - DOUBLE IPA W/ BOLD HOP AROMAS OF CITRUS PEEL AND PINE

RESERVE POURS   14oz - 8.00   MUG CLUB - 8.00   BEER TO GO   64oz/32oz   20/10

MICHIGANTIAN - DOUBLE IPA, BREWED W/ CHERRIES & PURELY-GROWN-IN-MICHIGAN INGREDIENTS

... VARIETIES OF MALT & ... BLACK CHERRIES

7.
6.
6.
8.
8.
8.
7.

SHO...

YOSEMITE SC...
BANG! American Pale-Ale B...
NOW ON
$5.99/6P

of this writing, there are thirteen breweries and brewpubs in the region—not bad for a town of fifteen thousand. Certainly, the tourists help support all the fine beer that's produced. "We are just inundated with visitors up here," Mike continued. "Lake Michigan has incredible blue water. It looks just like the Caribbean, without sharks. It used to be crowded just in the summer, but now we get people in the winter to cross-country ski and snowshoe."

With the many fruits that are cultivated around Grand Traverse Bay, it's no surprise that some make it into Traverse City beers. "Everyone does a cherry ale or cherry wheat beer at some point in the year, but fortunately none of them taste like cough syrup," Mike said. "A lot of hops are being grown now out on the Leelanau, and many brewers are using those local hops in IPAs, which is probably the most popular style." Beyond hops and cherries, Traverse City brewers have built a reputation for pushing the flavor envelope. "Jolly Pumpkin, out on Old Mission Peninsula, focuses on Belgian farmhouse ales," Mike added. "Dave Hale at North Peak is a great, creative brewer. He often has a cask ale on tap. Workshop always has solid beers on tap, and good food too. Right Brain is definitely worth a stop to see how insane Russell is. There's always interesting stuff on tap there." That's not an understatement; Right Brain brews over seventy beers in all, ranging from Broken Nose (a wet hopped double black IPA) to Cool Hand Cuke (a cucumber based saison) to Thai Peanut (a brown ale made with peanut butter, cilantro, serano peppers, and coconut oil).

Traverse City boasts a variety of pubs that showcase local product. "To get a great overview of what's brewing around Traverse City, you'll want to visit 7 Monks Taproom," Mike offered. "They have a massive tap selection [forty-six beers, mostly local]. The bar is well attended, so they churn through beer before it can go stale. There are a couple of older taverns that have a lot of character. Little Bohemia used to be pretty rough; all the tables are pedestals, so people couldn't throw them at each other. They have ten taps, all craft beer (except for PBR and Guinness). Another old tavern is Sleder's. It was a speakeasy during Prohibition. It's so old, there's a back room where only Native Americans were allowed; it was the only tavern that served Native Americans. It doesn't look like a craft beer spot, but the beer selection has gotten much better. Finally, there's the U and I, the second-oldest bar in Traverse City. It doesn't have a huge selection of taps, but there's a timelessness about the place . . . though it could be that they just don't clean it well."

OPPOSITE:
Short's Brewing is one of thirteen breweries in Greater Traverse City, an attractive resort town on Lake Michigan.

DESTINATION

31

The Lake Michigan shoreline—particularly to the west and south of Traverse City—is spectacularly beautiful and worthy of exploration . . . perhaps with a growler on ice. You can head out to the tip of the Leelanau Peninsula to Lighthouse Point, home of a beacon that was built more than 150 years ago. Just to the west is Sleeping Bear Dunes National Lakeshore—voted the most beautiful area in the United States by the viewers of ABC's *Good Morning America* in 2011. The reserve extends some thirty-five miles along the coast and showcases immense sand dunes perched atop towering headlands, the handiwork of steady winds from the west and glacial movement; some dunes, including Sleeping Bear itself, tower four hundred feet above Lake Michigan. The more adventurous will want to tackle the Dune Climb; after scaling the 110-foot high dune, many will roll back to the bottom. Inspiration Point, on the south side of Big Glen Lake, is a favorite place to toast the sunset; from the overlook, you can take in Glen Lake, the Crystal River, and the Dune Climb and gaze out across Lake Michigan to North Manitou Island. A little farther south is one of America's most celebrated open-to-the-public golf courses, Arcadia Bluffs. Modeled on the great links courses of Scotland and Ireland, the Bluffs unfolds over undulating fairways, vast sand traps, and almost constant views of the lake. Even if you hate golf, the setting is extremely dramatic. And the Lakeview Room—which delivers on its name—has eleven beers on tap, including Stormcloud Rainmaker, a Belgian pale ale from Stormcloud Brewing in nearby Frankfort.

MIKE HALL is a partner in Northern United Brewing Company, which encompasses North Peak Brewing, Grizzly Peak Brewing, Jolly Pumping Artisan Ales, Civilized Spirits, and Bonafide Wine. A world-renowned brewer, designer, and educator, he is a senior member of the European Institute and Guild of Brewing. Before becoming a partner in Northern United Brewing Company, Mike trained more than one hundred brewers. He has designed, built, and installed over forty breweries and distilleries around the globe, from as far away as Siberia to the Bahamas and several in Michigan. As managing partner of Northern United Brewing Company, Mike enjoys collaborating with Ron Jeffries, and together they have over fifty years of brewing experience and time at internationally renowned breweries such as Dogfish Head and Jolly Pumpkin.

DESTINATION

31

If You Go

▶ **Getting There:** Traverse City is served by several carriers, including American Eagle (800-433-7300; www.aa.com) and Delta (800-221-1212; www.delta.com).

▶ **Best Time to Visit:** Time your visit for your favorite outdoor activity. Traverse City Beer Week is held in mid-November.

▶ **Spots to Visit:** Rare Bird Brewpub (231-943-2053; www.rarebirdbrewpub.com); Jolly Pumpkin (231-223-4333; www.jollypumpkin.com); North Peak Brewing (231-941-7325; www.northpeak.net); Workshop Brewing (231-421-8977; www.traversecityworkshop.com); Right Brain Brewery (231-944-1239; www.rightbrainbrewery.com); 7 Monks Taproom (231-421-8410; www.7monkstap.com); Little Bohemia (231-946-6925; www.littlebohemia-tc.com); Sleder's (231-947-9213; www.sleders.com); U & I Lounge (231-946-8932; www.uandilounge.com); Arcadia Bluffs (800-494-8666; www.arcadiabluffs.com).

▶ **Accommodations:** The Park Place Hotel (231-946-5000; www.park-place-hotel.com) sits in the heart of the downtown area. Traverse City Tourism (800-872-8377; www.traversecity.com) lists other options.

DESTINATION

31

ST. LOUIS

RECOMMENDED BY **Pat Eby**

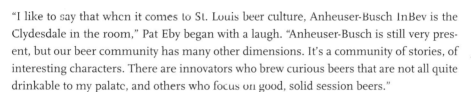

"I like to say that when it comes to St. Louis beer culture, Anheuser-Busch InBev is the Clydesdale in the room," Pat Eby began with a laugh. "Anheuser-Busch is still very present, but our beer community has many other dimensions. It's a community of stories, of interesting characters. There are innovators who brew curious beers that are not all quite drinkable to my palate, and others who focus on good, solid session beers."

OPPOSITE:
Urban Chestnut,
founded by
a former
Anheuser-Busch
brewer, mixes
older German
recipes with
contemporary
craft beer
styles.

There's no question that Anheuser-Busch's standard-bearer, Budweiser, has enjoyed better days, at least from a sales perspective. In 1988, nearly fifty million barrels of Bud were sold; in 2014, only sixteen million barrels were sold. One shouldn't feel too bad for AB; a good part of Bud's decline was absorbed by Bud Light drinkers, with Bud's lighter cousin becoming America's most popular beer in 2001. (Adolphus Busch arrived at the name Budweiser for his American-style lager in 1876, feeling it would appeal to German immigrants and at the same time could be easily pronounced by non-Germans. Innovations like pasteurization helped Bud be shipped far and wide and thus become a national brand.) That sixteen million barrels of Bud was eclipsed in 2015 by the output of small and independent brewers, which reached over twenty-two million barrels.

There's no question that craft brewers are becoming significant players in the American market—11 percent by volume and 19 percent by retail dollar value. Still, AB makes an awful lot of beer in its hometown of St. Louis, and they in turn play a visible role in the community. "Anheuser-Busch hosts many community events," Pat continued. "A favorite is Brewery Lights, which occurs during the winter holiday season. They have a beautiful complex of historic structures on the river. All the buildings are lit along the crenellated tops. They also have a walk-through tour with lighted billboard displays of old beer images, incredible lights, beer tastings, and fire pits, all complimentary; a gift to the community.

DESTINATION

32

"Two years ago, AB InBev opened a biergarten at the visitors' center in the brewery complex. If you happen to be there at three P.M., you can participate in a tasting—the same time the brewmasters are tasting beer in the brewery. It could be Budweiser or some other popular brand, or it could be a product that's not on the market. The brewmaster explains what he's looking for in the tasting."

On the brewery tours, they'll certainly offer people Bud and Busch, but they'll also share a few zingers from other brands in the portfolio to challenge people's tastes.

AB also holds beer-pairing dinners, called Table Talk, in conjunction with *St. Louis Magazine*. The dinners rotate at St. Louis's finest restaurants. George Reisch, the head brewmaster, usually presides, and he's a wonderful storyteller. He walks people through the beer styles and even shows people how to properly pour beer. One dinner that was especially popular was held the Libertine, where one course featured Goose Island's bourbon stout." [Goose Island was acquired by AB InBev in 2011.]

If AB InBev is the Clydesdale in the room, Earthbound Beer is in the room's closet—at one point, literally! "Earthbound started with a 1.5-barrel system that is housed in a closet," Pat described, "and the tasting room is in a hallway. They're moving to an eight-thousand-square-foot space, the old Cherokee Brewery, where they will run a seven-barrel system. Earthbound is doing some of the weirdest beers you could think of—like Dead Druid King, which uses oak leaves instead of hops as the bittering agent. I think they're up to nineteen different styles. But it's catching on. One distributor thinks they'll be on a hundred different taps within a year. There are three partners—the beer geek (Stuart Keating), who comes up with the recipes; the MacGyver guy (Jeff Siddons), who has constructed their pieced-together brewing systems; and the business person (Rebecca Schranz), who contributes to the beer recipes and keeps everything moving forward. The Cherokee Brewery used to have a large biergarten, and they are planning to bring that back."

If Earthbound is making its way to the big time, Urban Chestnut has already arrived. "Urban Chestnut is headed up by a former brewer from Anheuser-Busch, Florian Kuplent," Pat continued. "He does a mix of older German styles [the "Reverence" series] and more-contemporary craft beer styles [the "Revolution" series]. They took an old paper company space in a neighborhood called the Grove and reimagined it as a European-style bierhalle, with German-style food offerings. Many people from AB InBev are homebrewers, and they are big supporters of Urban Chestnut."

The list of interesting craft brewers in St. Louis goes on and on. Pat shared a few other favorites. "Phil Wymore at Perennial does a host of interesting beers. His brewery won a gold in 2015 at the Great American Beer Festival for Savant Blanc, a one-hundred-percent *Brettanomyces*-fermented ale aged in Chardonnay barrels with Chardonel grapes. Abraxas, an imperial stout [that's brewed with ancho chili peppers, cacao nibs, vanilla beans, and cinnamon sticks] received a ninety-seven rating from *BeerAdvocate* and sells out quickly. They do a Thursday-night tasting with experimental batches that they've collaborated on with homebrewers. The head brewer, Cory King, has a side project working on sour beers and saisons, fittingly called Side Project. In Lasalle Park, 4 Hands Brewery has a following for its stouts, and the artwork around its brands also gets high marks. Schlafly is the oldest craft brewery in St. Louis and the first since Prohibition, established in 1991. At one time they had a female brewer, Sara Hale. While Sara is no longer at the brewery, her husband, Stephen Hale, is Schlafly's beer ambassador. He's known for his stylish kilts, an everyday fashion. Schlafly's first location, the Tap Room, was a bombed out–looking building that was used as part of the dystopian set for the movie *Escape from New York*. They did a beautiful job renovating it. A smaller brewery named Heavy Riff was launched by two music-loving brothers, Justin and Jerid Saffell. Their flagship beer is a brown ale—Velvet Underbrown. They host vinyl nights with DJs; people can bring in their own records. There's Modern Brewery, which was started by a Harvard graduate named Beamer Eisele who crafted his own curriculum at Harvard around brewing. Later, he and his partner, Ronnie Fink, attended UC Davis to perfect their skills.

"If I only had one beer to enjoy in St. Louis, I think it would be at Civil Life. The owner, Jake Hafner, created a space well-tuned to a woman's experience. The tasting room is very laid back, so it's easy for a woman to come alone and sit at the bar. I'd order a Big Year Brown if available; if not, a Rye Pale Ale, which won a gold medal at the 2014 GABF. Bloomsday [a day-long reading and celebration of the James Joyce novel *Ulysses*] is a special time to visit."

PAT EBY is a freelance writer and designer based in St. Louis, where she writes about food, home, style, family, and health. Her writing has appeared in *St. Louis Magazine, St. Louis Post-Dispatch, Feast Magazine*, and *Sauce Magazine*. In her spare time, Pat enjoys gardening, drawing, and sewing and is a passionate reader.

If You Go

▶ **Getting There:** St. Louis is served by most major carriers.

▶ **Best Time to Visit:** You'll find the most temperate weather in the spring and fall. St. Louis Craft Beer Week (www.stlbeerweek.com) is held the last week in July.

▶ **Spots to Visit:** Budweiser Brew House (314-241-5575; www.stlballparkvillage.com/dining/dine/budweiser-brew-house); Earthbound Beer (314-769-9576; www.earthbound beer.com); Urban Chestnut (314-222-0143; www.urbanchestnut.com); Perennial Artisan Ales (314-631-7300; www.perennialbeer.com); Side Project Brewing (314-224-5211; www.sideprojectbrewing.com); 4 Hands Brewing (314-436-1559; www.4handsbrewery.com); Schlafly (314-241-2337; www.schlafly.com); Heavy Riff Brewing (www.heavyriffbrewing.com); Modern Brewery (www.modernbrewery.com); Civil Life Brewing (www.thecivillife.com). If you visit during the Christmas season, consider visiting Brewery Lights (www brewerylights.com).

▶ **Accommodation:** The St. Louis Convention & Visitors Commission (800-325-7962; www.explorestlouis.com) lists lodging options around the city.

DESTINATION

32

GLACIER NATIONAL PARK

RECOMMENDED BY **Sammi Johnson**

Lacking geysers, bison, and fumaroles, Glacier is perhaps destined to forever be Montana's second-best-known national park. But in terms of natural beauty, totemic wildlife (other than bison), and wide open spaces, Glacier is difficult to beat.

Glacier National Park comprises over one million acres in northwestern Montana, just to the east of the growing recreational region of Kalispell/Whitefish; the park abuts Alberta and contiguous Waterton Lakes National Park. Contrary to popular perception, the park is not named for existing glaciers (of which a few do remain), but for the work earlier glaciers did at the conclusion of the last ice age. These glaciers slowly scoured away deep valleys and sharp ridges, carving rugged mountains and deep lakes en route. Much of the high country in Glacier is above tree line. Since the mountains are actually a southern extension of the Canadian Rockies, they are more sedimentary in composition than the granitic American Rockies. The way these formations have worn away adds to their dramatic nature. Glacier is home to all of the big-game animals that were here when Lewis and Clark pushed west on a path south of the park in 1805—wolves, mountain lions, wolverines, lynx . . . and of course, grizzlies. The presence of these predators, especially the bears, lends any experience here more of a wilderness feeling, a little extra electricity.

"I grew up in Montana, near the town of White Sulphur Springs," Sammi Johnson began. "That's a few hours away from Glacier. But my family had a little cabin at Lake Five, just outside the border of the park, and I'd spend my summers there. I worked in the park right out of high school at the Glacier Park Boat Company. I continued working there during the summers while I was in college. I came back after college, found work nearby, and now am raising my family here in the Flathead Valley. It was a dreamland for a kid, and it still is for an adult.

"There are lots of places where I like to enjoy a beer in the park. It depends on whether I'm looking for an 'action beer' (where I'll have a beer while I'm participating in an activity) or an 'accomplishment beer' (where I'll have a beer to celebrate an achievement, like bagging a peak)." The hike to Iceberg Lake is one of Sammi's choices for an action beer. "Iceberg Lake is in the Many Glacier section of the park, on the east side," she continued. "Many Glacier is home to the immense Many Glacier Hotel, many activities, and it's a great place to access the back country." Iceberg Lake is considered one of the park's most scenic hikes—many rank it among the most scenic anywhere. The trail unfolds through open terrain, framed by Mount Wilbur in the background and the Ptarmigan Wall to the west, which towers nearly three thousand feet above the trail. Iceberg Lake is one of the gentler walks in Glacier, gaining a modest one thousand two hundred feet in elevation over roughly five miles. It's also a great trail for spotting grizzlies. (Bear spray is strongly advised.) Iceberg Lake itself is tucked back into a cirque, in the shadows of Mount Wilbur. It doesn't get a lot of sun, and the snow holds on for a long time, sometimes calving off the north shore to create small icebergs. "Iceberg Lake is amazingly blue," Sammi added. "There are large flat rocks along the edge that make great lunch spots. You can let your beer chill—in my case, almost always an IPA—in the lake a few minutes before you drink it. One local IPA I like is Cloudcroft from Kalispell Brewing Company. Once you finish the hike, you'll want to stop by the Many Glacier Hotel for an accomplishment beer. They have a huge back deck that looks out across Swiftcurrent Lake to Mount Grinnell. You can buy a craft beer inside or bring your own. There's no cell service, so you have to just be in the moment and enjoy the view. It's so expansive, you feel like you're in the biggest place in the world."

There are certainly ways to experience Glacier's grandeur with a bit less exertion. One is driving Going-to-the-Sun Road, which cuts fifty-two miles across the center of the park in a west-to-east direction. Frequently ranked among the world's most scenic roads, Going-to-the-Sun showcases many of the park's most iconic features, from glacial lakes to windswept passes—from the comfort of your car. Another route that better lends itself to a leisurely beer is taking a ride on one of the Glacier Park Boat Company's wooden boats. "Before Going-to-the-Sun Road was built in 1932, the boats were one of the only ways to enjoy the park," Sammi explained. "They were built in the early 1900s and require constant care. The biggest boat [the fifty-seven-foot-long DeSmet, named for a Jesuit missionary in the region] is on Lake McDonald at the west end of the park.

OPPOSITE:
Lake McDonald
is a great place
to enjoy a local
brew in Glacier
National Park.

DESTINATION

33

Hour-long tours are offered, and you can pick up a craft beer for the ride at Lake McDonald Lodge. Boat rides are also available on Swiftcurrent Lake and Lake Josephine at Many Glaciers, at St. Mary Lake, and at Two Medicine Lake. The deck of one these historic wooden boats is an amazing place to learn about the area and enjoy a beer."

One of Sammi's most memorable 'accomplishment beers' came after conquering the Skyline Trail, one of Glacier's more demanding day hikes. "Skyline is pretty much off trail," she described. "It begins near the Many Glacier Hotel, climbs up Wynn Mountain, and then travels six miles along a ridge until you reach Mount Siyeh, one of five peaks over ten thousand feet in the park. From there, you descend to Going-to-the-Sun Road. [The route is sixteen to eigtheen miles, depending on how you descend.] The ridge walk portion of the hike is extremely humbling. You never feel too exposed, but the views are endless. On this particular occasion I was hiking with my husband, and we had a grizzly encounter . . . not something I'll soon forget. We celebrated our hike—and the fact that we were still alive—at the Cattle Baron, a great steakhouse just east of the park. The power of nature we experienced on that hike reminded us that we aren't always in charge."

SAMMI JOHNSON is a native Montanan and a University of Montana graduate, where she studied marketing and recreation management. She is marketing director for the Flathead Beacon, which delivers thought-provoking news and commentary to Northwest Montana. Before coming to the Beacon, Sammi worked in public relations at Outside Media in Columbia Falls. An avid runner, hiker, and overall outdoors enthusiast, Sammi lives in the Flathead Valley with her husband, Tyrel, and their children, Savannah and Maddox.

DESTINATION 33

If You Go

▶ **Getting There:** Visitors can fly to Kalispell (twenty-five miles west of the park head-quarters), which is served by Alaska Airlines (800-252-7522; www.alaskaair.com) and United (800-864-8331; www.united.com). There's also Amtrak service to Glacier (800-872-7245; www.amtrak.com).

▶ **Best Time to Visit:** Peak season is June through September; October can be beautiful, but winter weather can blow in at any time. The Glacier National Park website (www.nps. gov/glac) lists conditions.

▶ **Spots to Visit:** Many Glacier Hotel; Lake McDonald Lodge; Glacier Park Boat Company (406-257-2426; www.glacierparkboats.com); Cattle Barron Supper Club (406-732-4033). En route to and from the park, consider stopping for a beer at Backslope Brewing (www. backslopebrewing.com) in Columbia Falls; Kalispell Brewing Company (406-756-2739; www.kalispellbrewing.com) in Kalispell; or Great Northern Brewing Company (406-863-1000; www.greatnorthernbrewing.com) in Whitefish.

▶ **Accommodations:** Reservations for Many Glacier Hotel, Lake McDonald Lodge, and other properties in the park can be made through Glacier National Park Lodges (855-733-4522; www.glaciernationalparklodges.com).

DESTINATION

33

LAKE LAS VEGAS

RECOMMENDED BY **Kate Fitzpatrick**

In a fine *New Yorker* magazine feature, writer and "Talk of the Town" editor Lizzie Widdicombe described how a trail run near Lake Tahoe suddenly turned into something different:

> Then, at a bend in the path, I heard whoops, and blood-curdling screams. It sounded like a village being attacked by marauding barbarians. In a clearing in the woods were two metal dumpsters, each eight feet wide and thirty feet long, filled with nine thousand gallons of melting ice, mixed with mud, to create a near-freezing slush. Ladders were propped up against the sides of them, and young people were lining up to jump in, as spectators cheered. . . .

As anyone who has considered participating in an endurance sport in recent years may recognize, Widdicombe was about to enter the Arctic Enema, one of the signature obstacles on the Tough Mudder.

"I was a bit nervous before my first Tough Mudder," Kate Fitzpatrick confessed. "I participated with twenty colleagues not long after I joined the company. The event was held on a mountain course in Vermont, at Mount Snow. The obstacles were intimidating, as was the steep nature of the course. But the team aspect of the event was phenomenal. And beer was definitely part of the experience at the finish line!"

Tough Mudder was founded by Will Dean and Guy Livingstone in 2010. Dean had completed dozens of marathons and triathlons and wished to create a team-based obstacle-event series that challenged physical and mental barriers but also encouraged people to work as a team to overcome obstacles together. The standard course is ten to twelve miles in length; camaraderie is more important than where participants place in

OPPOSITE: Participants in the Las Vegas Tough Mudder tangle with the "King of the Swingers." After completing this obstacle course/ endurance event, you've surely earned a beer!

DESTINATION

34

the rankings, and people of varying levels of fitness will participate. (The event is not timed.) The first event was held in Pennsylvania in 2010, and five hundred participants were expected. Nearly five thousand people showed up! Since that first event, more than two million people have participated in Tough Mudder events.

Wherever you live, chances are good there's a Tough Mudder coming to you soon. Events have been held from Sydney, Australia, to Whistler, British Columbia, and in or near many cities across the United States . . . including Las Vegas. "You need a lot of land to hold a Tough Mudder event," Kate explained. "We came upon such a piece of land—a real estate project that hasn't gotten off the ground—around Lake Las Vegas [a 320-acre artificial lake], which is only thirty minutes from the Vegas strip, in Henderson. It's a rugged course through a desert landscape with rolling hills and a few small mountains, with part of the course running along the oasis-like lake."

For many beer lovers, running (walking?) ten or twelve miles on a flat track would be more than enough exertion to feel justified in enjoying a few cold ones. In addition to a few hills and mountains, the Lake Las Vegas course includes Tough Mudder's trademark obstacles, designed to test both physical and mental strength. "Different people fear different things," Kate commented. "The obstacles play on people's fears, but then help them work through those fears. I don't like heights, so one of the new obstacles, King of the Swingers (which requires you to leap off a high platform to a rope swing dangling above a pit of water), terrifies me, but at the same time is exciting. Tough Mudder is always developing new obstacles and enhancing existing ones, but there are a few signature experiences that you can anticipate. One is Everest, which requires you to run up a slippery quarter pipe (like those used by skateboarders). This one's all about teamwork; ninety-nine percent of participants can't get up without help from their colleagues. Arctic Enema plays on your mental grit. You have to slide under a chain-link fence into ice-cold water, then climb over a wood partition in the middle and drop into the ice again. The shock is bracing; this is an obstacle that seems to require lots of mental preparation." Participants can take as long as they wish to complete the course. Some will finish in 1.5 hours, others will take five or six . . . and there's no shame in taking longer.

The beer component of a Tough Mudder challenge generally comes at the end of the race. Participants have certainly earned it. "I've done five Tough Mudders," Kate said, "and as I get toward the end, I'm always thinking about that beer. It's a motivator for me. Once you've conquered this amazing challenge, you want to celebrate." For the near

DESTINATION

34

future, the beer you'll be enjoying in the beer garden at the Lake Las Vegas event—or any other North American venue, for that matter—will be from Shock Top, which specializes in fruit-infused wheat beers and is a Tough Mudder sponsor. (Belgian White is Shock Top's most popular offering; others include Honeycrisp Apple Wheat, Raspberry Wheat, Lemon Shandy, Pumpkin Wheat, Shockolate Wheat, Twisted Pretzel Wheat, and Spiced Banana Wheat.) "It's a very celebratory environment, and very communal," Kate added. "People love to relive the obstacles and toast them with a beer."

The beer, by the way, is included in your entry fee.

KATE FITZPATRICK is the Senior Director of Community Development & Venues for Tough Mudder. She oversees the entire venue selection process and community relations for the company's North American events, scouting some of the most beautiful and unique locations imaginable. Kate studied art history at Middlebury College, which landed her in the legal office of the Metropolitan Museum of Art. She later went on to Brooklyn Law School and jumped into the startup scene as General Counsel and Director of Operations for a digital consulting firm before joining Tough Mudder.

If You Go

▶ **Getting There:** Las Vegas is served by most major carriers.
▶ **Best Time to Visit:** Tough Mudder (www.toughmudder.com) events are held spring/summer/fall throughout North America, as well as in Australia, Germany, the United Kingdom, and Ireland. The Lake Las Vegas event is generally held in October. Individual entry fees (as of this writing) are $195, but participants are encouraged to sign up as early as possible to get the best price.
▶ **Spots to Visit:** The beer garden past the finish line is the focus of most beer drinking at Tough Mudder events in Las Vegas. Vegas.com lists some recommended beer bars.
▶ **Accommodations:** The Tough Mudder website highlights hotel partners for each event. You'll also find an extensive list of lodging options at www.lasvegas.com.

DESTINATION

34

BENEDICTINE MONASTERY OF CHRIST IN THE DESERT

RECOMMENDED BY **Berkeley Merchant**

As most beer aficionados know, monasteries—particularly in Belgium—have played an essential role in the development and refinement of the brewing arts. The Trappist monks garner much of the attention as brewers, but you may not realize that the tradition started with the Benedictine order. The Benedictines are the oldest monastic order in Western Christianity, dating back to the beginning of the sixth century AD. Their inclination to brew beer stemmed in part from the monks' desire to have potable beverages to serve to their guests, as most freshwater sources of the time were tainted.

"Hospitality has always been a hallmark of Benedictine monasteries," Berkeley Merchant began. "Saint Benedict said that every visitor to a Benedictine monastery must be treated as if they were the Christ, no matter their spiritual tradition or station in life. Each guest is assured three things: safety (in days of yore, weapons were checked at the door); a place to sleep out of the elements; and sustenance. Another tenet of Benedictine monasteries is self-reliance. The Benedictines believe strongly in the dignity of work—a very novel idea in the sixth century, when manual work was for serfs and slaves. To be able to provide for themselves and for their guests, the monks needed to make a living. Today, the monks at the Benedictine Monastery of Christ in the Desert are no different. Historically, they've made their living through crafts—soaps, lotions, and leather goods—as well as by running guest houses for visitors. The idea of starting a brewery arose as another way to supplement the monastery's income."

The Christ in the Desert monastery sits some seventy-five miles north of Santa Fe, in the midst of some of New Mexico's most stunning high desert country. It's adjoined by the Chama River and the Chama River Canyon Wilderness. The multicolored sandstone canyons, shifting layers of red, cream, and brown, some soaring to heights over 1,500

OPPOSITE:
The ales that originated along the Chama River in New Mexico's high desert earned high praise from visiting Belgian monks.

DESTINATION

35

feet, make good on the state's slogan, "Land of Enchantment." Rafting enthusiasts have made the Chama River one of New Mexico's favorite floats; it's also a celebrated trout fishery. Given northern New Mexico's incredible color palette and play of light, it's no surprise that many painters have been drawn to the region. Perhaps none of the region's artists are better known than Georgia O'Keeffe. It was at Ghost Ranch—just up the road from Christ in the Desert—that Georgia O'Keeffe lived and painted during the latter years of her life (the Pedernal, a flat-topped mountain near the monastery, was one of her most painted landscapes).

About fifty monks, ranging in age from their early twenties to their nineties, from five different continents, form the monastic community at Christ in the Desert. "Community was very important to Saint Benedict, and a big part of a successful monastery is the ability of the brothers to get along," Berkeley continued. "I think this explains why the monks are so quiet and nonjudgmental. Each has his own foibles and has had to learn to put those aside to live closely and in harmony with others." The monks have a strict schedule, beginning with prayer services at four A.M. every day. There are six more services in the course of the day, plus time for work and contemplation. (Monks do not take a vow of silence, by the way; if visitors ask a question, the monks will respond. Their propensity for quiet might be explained by the aphorism "It's hard to hear the voice of God when you're talking.")

Established in 1964, the Monastery of Christ in the Desert did not begin Abbey Brewing Company until 2003. "One of the monastery's supporters, Dr. David A. Gonzalez of Santa Fe, provided the seed money to get the brewery going," Berkeley said, "and the first commercially available beer—Monks' Ale, a Belgian abbey single ale—was released in 2005. To develop this and other beers, Brad Kraus, a legendary New Mexican brewer, was recruited to be the brewmaster. For the first few years there was just the one beer— Monks' Ale—and it was available only in New Mexico. I became involved on the business side after moving down to Santa Fe from Oregon to escape the winter rain. Our goal remains to brew classic European monastic styles; it's been working for fourteen hundred years, so we thought we'd stick with it. Now, we have five core styles of beer—Monks' Ale, Monks' Dark Ale, Monks' Dubbel, Monks' Tripel, and Monks' Wit—with others on the way. And our beers are exported to five states. We grow some of our own hops, including a variety native to northern New Mexico and Colorado, Neomexicanus, which are used in our Reserve series of beers. We have a pilot brewery at the monastery—which is closed to the public—where we develop new beers. Several monks participate in the brewing process, working it in around their prayer life and other roles at the monastery. Most of the brewing occurs further south, in Moriarty, where we share equipment with Sierra Blanca Brewing. No matter where the beer is brewed, all our beers are made with care and prayer."

A visit to the Monastery of Christ in the Desert takes commitment. The monastery rests at the end of a thirteen-mile dirt road, though the drive in is like meandering through a series of O'Keeffe paintings. "When you're a mile and a half away, you come around a corner," Berkeley explained, "and you can make out the spire of the chapel that was designed by noted woodworker, architect, and furniture maker George Nakashima. It blends in so well with the natural landscape, it gives you goose bumps." Day visitors are welcome, as are overnight guests, for anywhere from two nights to two weeks. As a visitor, you can participate in prayer services and the monks' work duties as much or as little as you wish. Overnight guests receive three healthy meals. "Guests come for three reasons," Berkeley added. "The first is the natural beauty of the place. The second is the incredible quiet and solitude, something that's alien in our lives today. The third is the spiritual connection people feel in the valley and vicinity. Several other faith traditions have established faith-based retreat centers in the area around Abiquiú, Española, and Santa Fe."

It should be noted that Abbey Brewing ales are not available for purchase or tasting at the monastery. However, the ales are on tap (and available for takeaway in bottles) at Bode's General Store, a legendary northern New Mexico institution in Abiquiú and the nearest community to the Monastery of Christ in the Desert.

The Monastery of Christ in the Desert celebrated its fiftieth anniversary in 2014. To commemorate this milestone, visitors and other Benedictines from around the world came to partake in the festivities. "Several abbots from European monasteries, including Belgium, came to the Monastery of Christ in the Desert during the yearlong celebration," Berkeley recalled. "Naturally, they wanted to sample our beer. After a few tastes, one of the abbots said, 'This is as good as anything we have in Belgium. How much can I fit in my suitcase?'"

BERKELEY MERCHANT is an oblate of the Monastery of Christ in the Desert and also the general manager and assistant brewer of Abbey Brewing Company. Prior to moving to

New Mexico in 2006, he worked for twenty-eight years as a senior executive in several high-technology companies in Oregon.

If You Go

▶ **Getting There:** The town of Abiquiú and the Monastery of Christ in the Desert are roughly two hours north of Albuquerque, which has service from most major carriers.

▶ **Best Time to Visit:** Summers can be quite warm in the high desert around Abiquiú and Rio Chama, so many visitors prefer spring and early fall.

▶ **Spots to Visit:** While you can't drink or purchase beer at the Monastery of Christ in the Desert (575-613-4233; www.christdesert.org), a visit will nonetheless be rewarding. To partake of Abbey Brewing Company (www.abbeybrewing.biz), stop at Bode's (505-685-4422; www.bodes.com). The monks' ales will also be available in Albuquerque at the Monk's Corner, scheduled to open in 2016.

▶ **Accommodations:** If you don't opt to stay at the monastery, New Mexico Tourism (www.newmexico.org) highlights options near Abiquiú or further south in Santa Fe and Albuquerque.

BROOKLYN

RECOMMENDED BY **Steve Hindy**

Back in the late nineteenth century, Brooklyn—the most populated of New York's five boroughs—generated 10 percent of the beer brewed in America. By the time Steve Hindy arrived back in New York in 1984 after five years in the Middle East as a correspondent with Associated Press, Brooklyn's last two breweries (Schaeffer and Rheingold) had been shuttered for eight years. "There were two microbreweries that began operating in Manhattan in the mid-eighties," Steve recalled, "New Amsterdam and Manhattan Brewing Company, which was a brewpub. Matthew Reich of New Amsterdam was really a pioneer in the east, ahead of his time. He was contract brewing his beers upstate. They were doing quite well, but their financing fell through, and soon they were out of business. By the time we were ready to start brewing in 1988, we recognized that it made good business sense to contract brew.

"About that time I met Sophia Collier, who had great success with Soho Natural Soda, and asked for her advice. She liked the beer and the label (which had been designed by the legendary graphic designer Milton Glaser) but told me that it wouldn't succeed unless we distributed it ourselves; traditional distributors wouldn't work, as they wouldn't know what to do with the dark, hoppy beer we had. 'Distribute beer in New York?' I said. 'I can barely afford car insurance. What about parking tickets? The Mafia?' But her argument made sense. It wasn't easy to distribute beer, but it helped us get to know the business from the sales side and gain a foothold. We also began distributing quality beers from Belgium, Germany, Scandinavia, and even other American craft brands, like Sierra Nevada. Our distribution work helped establish the market for craft beer in New York."

By 1996, now famous brewmaster Garrett Oliver had joined the team, and demand had made it prudent for Brooklyn Brewery to build their own brewing facility. They chose

a site in the Williamsburg neighborhood. "On the day we opened—May 28—Mayor Rudy Giuliani came to cut the ribbon. The street was blocked off, and there must have been a hundred reporters in the audience. I introduced the mayor, and he pulled me next to him and said, 'I want all you journalists to look at this man. He used to be a reporter, but now he is making an honest living.' Then he joined the team in pouring beer for everyone. It turns out that the twenty-eighth was also the mayor's birthday." Today, there are over thirty breweries in New York City, with at least one in each borough. And every distributor wants craft brands as part of their offering.

There are countless beer bars in Brooklyn where you can enjoy a Brooklyn Lager or East IPA among the hipsters. Steve prefers a few spots that overlook that *other* borough and are perfect for a sunset beer. "Right across from the brewery is the Wythe Hotel," he continued. "They have an indoor bar with an outdoor terrace on the sixth floor, with breathtaking views of Manhattan. This is one of the great vistas in New York; you can watch the sun set behind Manhattan, see the lights come up as the sun goes down. There's a certain point where the lights of the city are brighter than the sun. Another spot is in the new Brooklyn Bridge Park, which runs from the Manhattan Bridge all the way around Brooklyn to Atlantic Avenue, along the East River. [The park rests on the site of a defunct cargo shipping and storage complex.] On Pier Six, there's a seasonal pizza restaurant called Fornino. There's an indoor restaurant on the ground level and a deck on the roof. Sitting up on the deck at a picnic table with a fabulous pizza and a Brooklyn beer is a world-class experience. If you want a romantic beer experience, consider the River Café. It's on a barge under the Brooklyn Bridge. You get a similar view as you do from the Wythe, but with the bridge soaring above and the Statue of Liberty in the distance."

Suffice it to say, Brooklyn has changed a bit in the last few decades. Today, you're more likely to encounter an artisan moccasin maker than a mobster . . . but in the mid-nineties, things were a bit different. Steve elaborated: "When we were starting to build the current brewery, the *Daily News* did a big centerfold story with photos of me and Garrett and the construction, as this would be the first brewery in Brooklyn in twenty years. The next day, two limos pulled up, and out stepped a couple characters right out of *Goodfellas*. Each had a bodyguard, and there were a couple of other cars with assorted thugs. All the construction workers disappeared, like rats off a doomed ship. The bosses wanted to chat with the guy in charge. I was out at lunch, so they left a card with a name for me to call. I went to the contractor and explained the visit. He said, 'Why did you get that article in the paper?

OPPOSITE:
New brewers face many challenges; when Brooklyn Brewery decided to build its own facility, those included local mobsters wanting a piece of the action.

DESTINATION

36

This is going to be a problem.' I handed the card to the contractor and asked him to return the call.

"A few days later, I get a call from an unfamiliar voice—'How come you didn't call my boss?' I stalled and then phoned the contractor and asked if he returned the call. He said I needed to do it. In the meantime, no one had shown up for work the last few days. I called a friend who had once been head of the organized-crime strike force for southern New York and asked what I should do. He said, 'You'd better talk to them, or else they might burn your place down or beat up your people.' 'What do they want?' I asked. 'Probably some no-show jobs.' I didn't want to do that—where would it ever stop? I asked what would happen if I called the prosecutor. He said they might ask me to wear a wire . . . and that I might have to eventually think about the witness-protection program. That wasn't going to go over well with my family. So I made the call.

"The two bosses showed up with assorted thugs, and they wanted to talk. My office was too crowded, so we went out to the warehouse and sat down in some broken office chairs. I started spilling my heart with stories about the Middle East. Their second in command—a stand-in for Joe Pesci—was restless, but the big boss told him to let me talk. Finally he says, 'We don't want to hurt you, but no one will come to work until we put the word out.' I continued talking, and eventually they went off to talk among themselves. I could hear them yelling at each other and I was beginning to sweat. The boss comes back and says he's going to have to hurt me. He walks me outside and slams me into a chain link fence. The he starts to laugh, and proceeds to invite me to his Christmas party. 'Bring your wife!' he said.

"I got to thinking about this guy a few years later, wondering if he and his gang were really bad guys. I Googled his name. He had been sent to prison for extortion on a school project not far from my home."

STEVE HINDY is cofounder and chairman of the Brooklyn Brewery, and a former Middle East correspondent for the Associated Press. He is a longtime member and past chairman of the board of directors of the Brewers Association. Steve is a former member of the board of the Beer Institute, the large brewers trade association. He is coauthor of *BEER SCHOOL*, written with cofounder Tom Potter, and *The Craft Beer Revolution*, an insider's look at the stunning growth of American craft beer. Steve has contributed to the *New York Times* and Vice Media, and has written for CNN and other publications. He also

DESTINATION

36

serves on the boards of Brooklyn's Prospect Park Alliance, the Open Space Alliance for North Brooklyn, and Transportation Alternatives.

If You Go

▶ **Getting There:** New York is served by all major carriers.

▶ **Best Time to Visit:** The outside tables at Wythe Hotel and Fornino are best enjoyed spring through fall. New York Beer Week is held the last week in February.

▶ **Spots to Visit:** Brooklyn Brewery (718-486-7422; www.brooklynbrewery.com); Wythe Hotel (718-460-8000; www.wythehotel.com); Fornino @ Brooklyn Bridge Park (718-422-1107; www.fornino.com); River Café (718-522-5200; www.therivercafe.com). The Brooklyn Brewery website features a list of the brewer's favorite Brooklyn beer bars.

▶ **Accommodations:** Explore Brooklyn (www.explorebk.com) lists lodging options around the borough.

WELLINGTON

RECOMMENDED BY **Angela Brownie**

The charming ocean-side city of Wellington is the capital of New Zealand. In many ways it calls to mind a smaller San Francisco—contained in the west by steep hills, to the east by Oriental Bay, very light and airy and very walkable. In recent years, Wellington has emerged as the beer capital of New Zealand as well . . .

"Wellington is a very eclectic city, extremely open-minded," Angela Brownie observed. "There are many creative people here—you can be anything you want to be. I think this open-mindedness has extended to the city's brewing culture. There's been a food and coffee culture here for a while. My sense is that the same people who supported those movements have been eager to support an innovative beer scene."

Not so long ago, Wellingtonian pubgoers (and for that matter, New Zealanders in general) had two beer options—products from Lion and products from DB. Like many pubs in the United Kingdom, brewers traditionally subsidized the cost of tap systems and hence controlled what flowed from those taps. If you visited a Lion house, it was probably Steinlager and perhaps a Speight's product; DB houses served DB Bitter, DB Draught, DB Export, and maybe a Monteith's brew. Opportunities began to unfold for smaller Wellington brewers when a new generation of publicans decided to go independent. "Some of our breweries are starting to have tasting rooms," Angela continued, "but for the most part, they are not set up to accommodate customers. In Wellington, beer lovers looking for something different go to independent bars. And most of these places are tucked away down alleyways and other out-of-the-way corners of the city. There's a sense of adventure in trying to locate these spots."

Angela traces the evolution of Wellington's close-knit craft beer scene to a handful of brewers, whom she went on to describe. "A fellow named Carl Vasta led the charge, starting

OPPOSITE:
Beer lovers
visiting
Wellington's
pubs (like
Golding's Free
Dive) will find a
warm, inviting
atmosphere.

Tuatura. Carl traveled the world when he was younger and spent time in England, where he was taken with the beer. He wanted to emulate the beers he sampled there back in his native New Zealand and eventually started Tuatara. The brewery, which is one of Wellington's largest, is named for a New Zealand reptile that's believed to be the closest living relative to the dinosaurs. Their bottles have ridges like those on the lizard's back. One of his noteworthy brews is Sauvinova, a single-hop ale made with Nelson Sauvin hops, which are grown near the town of Nelson on the South Island.

"Other key players include Jos Ruffell, Mike Neilson, Stu McKinlay, and the three Matts (Warner, Kristofski, and Stevens). Jos started Garage Project in an old petrol station as a true nanobrewery. When he opened in 2011, he served twenty-four different beers in twenty-four days, at the same time each day, in a very limited quantity. Garage Project pushes the flavor boundary with ingredients like juniper and chile—not for the faint of heart. One of their recipes, Sauvin Nouveau, combines pilsner wort and Sauvignon Blanc. Mike Neilson is a hot-rod enthusiast who learned to brew at Tuatura and now plies his trade at Panhead Brewery. Panhead's brands are built around car imagery, and their can and bottle designs are as distinctive as their beers. They make one of my favorite Wellington beers, a hefeweizen called Herman Holeshot that's just exquisite. Stu McKinlay, who started Yeastie Boys in 2009 with Sam Possenniskie, has emerged as a pinup boy for Wellington craft brewing. Yeastie Boys' first brew, Pot Kettle Black, won a number of awards. One of their recent concoctions is Gunnamatta IPA, an IPA that's 'dry leafed' with Earl Grey Blue Flower tea. Two of the ParrotDog Matts [Warner and Kristofski] started brewing together as students. Their first brewing gig was a contract beer for someone else. The client didn't care for the ale's bitterness, but many others did, and BitterBitch was born."

The next logical question is, of course, where to go to enjoy some of Wellington's best beers. Angela shared a few of her favorites. "Golding's Free Dive is a must-visit. They have an excellent selection of local taps and attract a very diverse clientele that's very representative of the city. Hashigo Zake Cult Beer Bar is another favorite. They constantly rotate the taps and also feature some fine ales from other countries. The Rogue & Vagabond has almost twenty local beers on tap and is also a great live-music venue. Tuatura has been so successful that they've opened their own pub, Third Eye, that's certainly worth a stop. The Garage Project is soon opening up their own pub as well." Wellington is big enough to be cosmopolitan, but small enough to be familiar. "Instead of talking about six degrees of separation, we talk about two degrees," Angela added. "There's a saying here: Go to a place once, they're friendly; go a second time, you're a mate; go a third time, they know your name."

ANGELA BROWNIE is general manager for business growth at Grow Wellington, where she oversees ongoing work alongside established businesses in a variety of market sectors, including manufacturing, clean technology, food and beverage, screen and digital, and information and communications technology (ICT). She has held senior management roles with Sleepyhead, Pacific Brands Homewares (Fairydown), Dexion Commercial New Zealand Ltd. (Precision), and Design Mobel. Angela has lived in Japan and the United States, where she studied e-commerce in New York before returning to study commercial law at Victoria University.

If You Go

▶ **Getting There:** International travelers can reach Wellington by Air New Zealand (800-262-1234; www.airnewzealand.com) and Jetstar (866-397-8170; www.jetstar.com) via Auckland and Christchurch.

▶ **Best Time to Visit:** February and March boast Wellington's finest weather, though the climate is temperate year-round.

▶ **Spots to Visit:** Golding's Free Dive (+64 4 381 3616; www.goldingsfreedive.co.nz); Hashigo Zake Cult Beer Bar (+64 4 384 7300; www.hashigozake.co.nz); Rogue & Vagabond (+64 4 381 2321; www.rogueandvagabond.co.nz); the Third Eye (+64 04 803 3948; www.tuatarabrewing.co.nz). A comprehensive list of pubs and breweries resides at www.craftbeercapital.com.

▶ **Accommodations:** A comprehensive list of accommodations is available from Positively Wellington Tourism (+64 4 802 4860; www.wellingtonnz.com).

DESTINATION

37

ASHEVILLE

RECOMMENDED BY **Hilton Swing**

Asheville, North Carolina, is an eclectic small city in the Blue Ridge Mountains of west-ern North Carolina where new agers, outdoor enthusiasts, musicians, and local-food advocates all coexist under a patina of Southern charm. There's a progressive, hip vibe here that some might not expect in southern Appalachia. Thanks to its elevation (2,134 feet above sea level), Asheville avoids the intensive heat one might associate with a Carolina summer.

"Asheville has had a great tourism base for many years," Hilton Swing observed. "We are a gateway to the Great Smokies and the Blue Ridge Mountains and have the Biltmore Estate. The growth of the beer scene here has been a great addition for visitors. It's become part of the tourism experience. Like our food movement, there's a great appeal attached to the idea of a local product. With the Asheville Ale Trail, we've tried to focus on the overall experience and keep things accessible to someone who might not yet be a beer aficionado but wishes to learn more."

Asheville now boasts more than a dozen breweries and a number of fine tap houses featuring local product. It all started in 1992 when an engineer named Oscar Wong, who had specialized in designing nuclear waste facilities, decided to retire in Asheville. As a hobby, he started a small brewery in the basement of an existing taproom and called it Highland Brewing, a nod to Asheville's Scotch/Irish heritage. The brewery produced its first beer in 1994; today, Highland produces forty thousand barrels per annum and is distributed in thirteen states. "The industry really wouldn't be what it is in Asheville with-out Oscar's guidance and pleasant demeanor," Hilton continued.

If you want a crash course in the Asheville brewing culture, you could do worse than spending an afternoon and/or evening strolling around the city's South Slope neighborhood.

OPPOSITE:
Wicked Weed is
one of more than
a dozen breweries
in Asheville, a
western North
Carolina town
that's a hub
for outdoor
enthusiasts and
foodies alike.

DESTINATION

38

"Asheville is built on a knoll," Hilton explained, "with the core city on top. The South Slope was once the warehouse district, but the breweries have moved in. There are eight that are all within a mile's walk—Asheville Brewing Company, Hi-Wire Brewing, Twin Leaf Brewery, Green Man Brewery, Burial Beer, Catawba Brewing, Wicked Weed Brewing, and Wicked Weed Funkatorium. Asheville Brewing is one of the originals; they opened not long after Highland. [Asheville Brewing has three locations in town; their Merrimon Avenue pub offers a movie theater. Asheville Brewing will also deliver beer to your door!] Catawaba is another of the older breweries and also has three locations. Burial Beer started as a nanobrewery but now has a ten-barrel system.

"Wicked Weed opened in 2012, and they quickly built a loyal following. They renovated an old art deco building, putting a restaurant on top and a fifteen-barrel brewery and taproom in the bottom. Overall, they raised the bar for Asheville." In the taproom, up to twenty-five beers will be flowing at a given time, split roughly between more hop-forward, American-style ales and Belgian-style beers and sours. Wicked Weed Funkatorium has the distinction of being the East Coast's first dedicated sour beer and barrel-aged beer tasting room, with a dozen or more beers flowing. Inspired by the Belgian brewing process of spontaneous fermentation, sour beers are created by introducing bacteria and wild [as opposed to brewer's] yeasts to fermenting beer . . . and seeing what happens. The result is [generally] a tart, sour, and engagingly [at least for some] complex beverage that bears little resemblance to traditional ales or lagers. "I would say that the local market here has a diverse and sophisticated palate," Hilton opined. "The sour beers that Wicked Weed is doing have become popular, but so are saisons and IPAs. The bottom line is that brewers can't get by with just five beers. They have to step up their game to compete in Asheville."

One of the most telling signs that Asheville has truly arrived on the craft brewery scene has been the recent opening of East Coast outposts of several western craft brewing powerhouses. These include New Belgium (brewers of Fat Tire Amber Ale, from Colorado), Oskar Blues (brewers of Dale's Pale Ale and canned craft beer pioneer, also from Colorado), and Sierra Nevada (from California). "It was pretty spectacular that these brands chose the Asheville region, as there were many other places they could've gone," Hilton said. "I think the outdoors-oriented culture here was a good match, and Asheville is already a craft beer–friendly environment—plus, the local brewing community has been very accepting. The Sierra Nevada brewery is set a bit outside of town, in Mills River.

It provides an amazing visitor experience from the beginning: You crest a hill, and there's the brewery in all its glory. They have a one-hundred-eighty-acre campus. The brewery has a fairly small footprint; there's an amphitheater for live music and walking trails. The brewery tours are very well laid out. One tour focuses on the brewing facility, another highlights Sierra's sustainability initiatives. There's an outdoor space where kayakers from the river can pull up and stop in for a meal or a few beers. If you're in town for a few days, you should definitely spend one evening out in Mills River. The New Belgium facility, which is being built in town, will have many of the same characteristics. It's being constructed on a brownfield site, part of the company's environmental commitment."

HILTON SWING is a not-often-enough traveler, occasional writer, and entrepreneur. He believes that the experience you have while drinking beer is every bit as important as what's inside the bottle. Hilton is the founder of the Asheville Ale Trail (www.asheville aletrail.com).

If You Go

▶ **Getting There:** Asheville is served by a number of carriers, including American (800-433-7300; www.aa.com); Delta (800-221-1212; www.delta.com), and United (800-864-8331; www.united.com).

▶ **Best Time to Visit:** May through October, with fine foliage displays in the fall. Various beer festivals are held throughout the year. Brewgrass (www.brewgrassfestival.com), a popular music/beer event, is held each year in mid-September.

▶ **Spots to Visit:** Highland Brewing (828-299-3370; www.highlandbrewing.com); Asheville Brewing (828-255-4077; www.ashevillebrewing.com); Burial Beer (828-475-2739; www.burialbeer.com); Wicked Weed Brewing (828-575-9599; www.wickedweed brewing.com); Wicked Weed Funkatorium (828-552-3203); Sierra Nevada Brewing Company (828-708-6242; www.sierranevada.com). The Asheville Ale Trail (www.asheville aletrail.com) lists a host of walking/riding tours and lists Asheville's best beer bars.

▶ **Accommodations:** You'll find a comprehensive list of lodging options at www.explore asheville.com.

BEND

RECOMMENDED BY **Gary Fish**

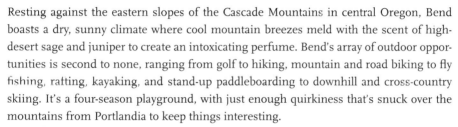

Resting against the eastern slopes of the Cascade Mountains in central Oregon, Bend boasts a dry, sunny climate where cool mountain breezes meld with the scent of high-desert sage and juniper to create an intoxicating perfume. Bend's array of outdoor opportunities is second to none, ranging from golf to hiking, mountain and road biking to fly fishing, rafting, kayaking, and stand-up paddleboarding to downhill and cross-country skiing. It's a four-season playground, with just enough quirkiness that's snuck over the mountains from Portlandia to keep things interesting.

And, Bend has one of the highest breweries per capita in the country!

"Bend is very much a lifestyle community," Gary Fish began. "People come to vacation, and a fair amount end up staying. You might argue that people who live and work here are always on vacation! Bend has changed a great deal since I moved here in 1987. Then, it was twelve thousand or fifteen thousand people. Now it's over eighty thousand. But the priorities are still geared toward quality of life. I don't know anyone who lives here for the money, because you can make more money somewhere else. But there's a terrific energy here and a great quality of life.

For longtime central Oregonians who remember Bend as a modest timber town along the Deschutes River (the name comes from a prominent "bend" in the river), its incarnation as a beer mecca must be as mind-boggling as its transformation to an outdoor recreation hub. Bend now boasts twenty-one brewing concerns within its city limits, with another seven in surrounding towns. It all started in 1987 when Gary and his wife, Carol, took a trip to Bend from their home in Salt Lake City and liked what they saw. With encouragement from his father, who had worked in the wine industry in California and saw the business potential for brewpubs, Gary opened Deschutes Brewery in 1988 in

OPPOSITE:
The Cycle Pub is
one way to tour
downtown Bend's
many brewpubs.

DESTINATION

39

then quiet downtown Bend. Not long after opening, Gary received a call from a distributor in Portland interested in stocking Deschutes beers—at that time, Mirror Pond Pale Ale, Black Butte Porter, and Obsidian Stout. Soon, Deschutes was unable to make enough beer to cater to its brewpub customers. Today, Deschutes brews most of its beer at a state-of-the-art facility on the banks of its namesake river, produces over twenty styles, and is among the largest craft brewers in the country.

Being a part of the Bend community has always been an important goal for Gary and Deschutes Brewery. Beyond its support of local charities, Deschutes has done a great deal to create the "beervana" that Bend is today. "We were the first brewery here, and we are the largest," Gary continued. "Many of the people who have worked for us have eventually wanted to do something on their own. I did the same thing, so I certainly understand the urge and have never begrudged anyone leaving to pursue a different opportunity. Indirectly, we've populated a lot of breweries in the area . . . and others came because they liked the scene that's evolved in Bend."

Though farmhouse ales and sour beers are beginning to appear around Bend, the defining style is still India pale ale. Boneyard Beer's RPM, 10 Barrel Brewing's Apocalypse IPA, and Deschutes's Fresh Squeezed IPA are all good standard bearers. Crux Fermentation Project contributes an eminently drinkable session IPA to the mix. There are many fine spots where you can enjoy a beer. You could do worse than a visit to the Deschutes Public House, which generally has nineteen taps flowing and imaginative pub grub. Both 10 Barrel and Old St. Francis School (an outpost of the Portland-based McMenamins beer empire) have attractive fire pits where you can enjoy a libation outside during cooler weather. To facilitate your journey around town, the Bend Visitor Center has created the Bend Ale Trail. If your feet get tired, there are several companies that lead beer-inspired tours . . . or you can reserve a seat on the Cycle Pub, a trolley-like contraption that's powered by the pedaling of its occupants.

With the plentitude of great outdoor experiences within an hour's drive of downtown Bend, it can be difficult to nail down which pastime you should pursue first. A number of traditional triathlon events are held each spring and summer in the region, but it's also quite possible to construct your own triathlon. Gary shared one of his favorites. "My avocations revolve around golf and fly fishing, though I also enjoy skiing. In the springtime, you can combine all three. I'll head up to Mount Bachelor in the morning for some spring skiing. I'll leave late morning so I'm back down to Bend by noon. Then I'll play eighteen holes of golf. [The Bend region boasts over twenty-five courses.] I'll grab an early dinner, and then grab my fly rod to wet a line for trout on the Deschutes River, right in the middle of town. To top off the perfect day, I'll have a pint of Bachelor Bitter at the Deschutes Public House."

GARY FISH founded Deschutes Brewery in 1988 as a small downtown brewpub in Bend. Under his guidance, the brewery has grown over the years to encompass another brewpub in Portland, Oregon's Pearl District and a main brewing facility that produced more than 335,000 barrels of beer in 2014. The brewery, which was recently ranked as seventh largest in the country, distributes to twenty-eight states, the District of Columbia, and around the world. Over the years, Gary has guided the company to create award-winning beers all the way to creating an award-winning work environment—Deschutes Brewery was named one of *Outside Magazine*'s Best Places to Work for three years in row: 2013, 2014, and 2015. He is a recipient of the Oregon Restaurant Association's "Community Service" award and "Restaurateur of the Year" award, received the Governors' Gold Awards Program Al and Pat Reser Civic Leadership Award, and won the regional Ernst & Young Entrepreneur of the Year Award.

If You Go

▶ **Getting There:** Visitors can fly into nearby Redmond, Oregon, which is served by Alaska (800-252-7522; www.alaskaair.com) and Delta Airlines (800-221-1212; www.delta.com). Portland, which is served by most major carriers, is roughly 3.5 hours' drive.
▶ **Best Time to Visit:** The Bend Brewfest (www.bendbrewfest.com) is held each August.
▶ **Spots to Visit:** Deschutes Brewery (541-385-8606; www.deschutesbrewery.com); Deschutes Public House (541-382-9242; www.deschutesbrewery.com); Boneyard Beer (541-323-2325; www.boneyardbeer.com); 10 Barrel Brewing (541-678-5228; www.10barrel.com); Crux Fermentation Project (541-385-3333; www.cruxfermentation); Cycle Pub (541-678-5051; www.cyclepub.com).
▶ **Accommodations:** Guests at McMenamins Old St. Francis School (541-382-5174; www.mcmenamins.com/OldStFrancis) have a brewery on premises. Other options are highlighted at Visit Bend (877-245-8484; www.visitbend.com).

DESTINATION

39

HOOD RIVER

RECOMMENDED BY **Maui Meyer**

"If there's a theme for Hood River, it's back-pocket adventure," Maui Meyer began. "This area of the Columbia Gorge is a lost corner of the United States that just happens to be only sixty miles from a major metro area. There are thousands of old trails that you can hike on; in thirty minutes you can be in your own world. There's all the history in the town of The Dalles [which was the end of the Oregon Trail and an important meeting place for the Native American tribes along the Columbia River] just upriver. The area has this sense of raw abundance, with thriving farms and orchards. It's all so close. Then, when you hit Hood River, there's an interesting mixture of forward-thinking people. And so much good beer."

Hood River rests near the eastern edge of the Columbia Gorge, a remarkable canyon that was scoured to depths approaching four thousand feet by the Missoula Floods some thirteen thousand to fifteen thousand years ago. Driving from Portland, you'll notice a dramatic transition in the Gorge's flora as you head east; temperate rainforests of Douglas fir and western hemlock punctuated by cascading waterfalls (Multnomah Falls is the highest, at six hundred twenty feet) slowly give way to patches of Ponderosa pine and then grasslands as average precipitation dips from seventy-five to one hundred inches in the west to ten to fifteen inches in the east. (Considering the views, it's no wonder that railroad executive Sam Hill championed the building of the Columbia River Highway, which was built to showcase modern road design and building techniques, in 1915.) The town of Hood River, in the shadow of Mount Hood (elevation 11,250 feet and home to several ski areas) to the south and Mount Adams (elevation 12,280 feet) to the north and bordered on the east by its eponymous river and the Columbia, was once a sleepy orchard town, famous for its Anjou pears. It so happens that the shape of the gorge here acts as a

OPPOSITE:
Hood River
evolved from a
sleepy orchard
town to a mecca
for windsurfers
(and, later,
kiteboarders).
A number
of breweries
materialized to
slake outdoor
recreationalists'
thirst.

DESTINATION

40

wind tunnel, creating very consistent breezes, especially in the summer months. When the sport of windsurfing began gaining momentum in the early 1980s and "boardheads" discovered those steady twenty- to thirty-mile-per-hour winds, the seeds of Hood River's metamorphosis were sown.

"In the mid-1980s, I was traveling on the windsurfing world tour," Maui recalled. "The competitions were held in the spring and fall; in between, I worked for a national sailboard distributor and went from venue to venue to venue. Hood River was one of those stops. I remember flying into Portland and driving my team members out through the gorge at night. They were disgruntled at the long drive. We fell asleep in the campground; when we woke up, everyone was, 'Wow! We're in a special place.' This was in 1984, and I was eighteen—but I knew then that I would somehow figure out a way to return to Hood River, if only to retire. I finished my pro career and college, and an opportunity rose. By 1991, I was here."

The launch of Full Sail Brewing conveniently preceded Maui's return. Founder Irene Firmat and brewmaster Jamie Emmerson took possession of a long-abandoned Diamond Fruit cannery in 1987 and began converting the apple-juice press room into a brewhouse. Their first year's production—two hundred eighty-seven barrels—was well-received by Hood River's windsurfing arrivistes. Soon after, Hood River Brewing Company (it would later become Full Sail) began bottling its beer—a practice unheard of at that time for small brewers. They adapted a used Italian bottling line (made for wine), and began packaging Full Sail Golden Ale, Top Sail Imperial Porter, Full Sail Amber Ale, and Wassail Winter Ale. The amber became Full Sail's bestselling brew, garnering a gold medal at the 1989 Great American Beer Festival. In 1999, Full Sail would realize another milestone—becoming an employee-owned company, thus sharing the brewery's good fortunes with its (then) forty-seven employees.

Some things have changed in Hood River since Full Sail first bottled its Golden Ale. Windsurfing has largely been usurped by kiteboarding (which Maui equates to wakeboarding, with the power of the wind subbing in for the power of the boat), and Full Sail is no longer the only game in town when it comes to craft brewing . . . though it's still hard to beat the view of the Columbia from the deck of the Full Sail pub. Double Mountain Brewery, right around the corner from Full Sail, has quickly built a dedicated following, primarily on the strength of its hop-forward offerings, Hop Lava IPA and IRA (India Red Ale). The pub features excellent New Haven–style pizza and a solid soundtrack and is a favorite local hangout; skiers/snowboarders in the winter, kiteboarders, mountain bikers, and anglers in the summer. (If you happen to visit in the fall, the double-hopped Killer Green is not to be missed.) Near the banks of the Columbia you'll find pFriem, which successfully fuses northwest and Belgian ale styles to create memorable pours like its Blonde IPA; their menu does the same, applying local ingredients to Belgian favorites. Logsdon Farmhouse Ales and Big Horse Brew Pub round out the current lineup . . . more are on the way. "Our beer scene is getting ever more artisanal and intriguing," Maui added. "My tasting profile is becoming more wine-oriented, focusing on flavor, aromatics, finish. Some of these beers are complex pieces of art."

Though his competitive days are a bit behind him, Maui and his peers are still drawn to the river. "We all have kids now, and they have taken up kiteboarding," Maui said. "In the summer, there's a big sandbar on the river in front of town where we'll take them to kite. We'll bring chairs out. Someone will bring a six pack or a growler of good beer. Another guy will bring a ripe avocado with chips and salsa. We'll sit there and take in three-hundred-and-sixty-degree views of the gorge while the kids zip around and the sun slowly sets to the west."

MAUI MEYER found Hood River, Oregon, in 1985 as part of the Windsurfing World Tour. He immediately fell in love with the Hood River area and returned to live full-time in the Columbia Gorge in 1991, after graduating from Cornell University, in Ithaca, New York, where he studied food and beverage management, finance, and real estate development. "Post-college, Hood River had a strong draw, and it literally came down to making a choice about love of a place over the ability to earn a living," Maui said. "It was a great decision." In 1991, he opened the Sixth Street Bistro. A few years later, with additional partners, he began a construction company, Nisei; then Copper West and Oregon Growers and Shippers; and most recently, Celilo Restaurant and Bar. Maui is a Hood River county commissioner and is active in local and state politics, focusing on rural resource issues. He currently lives in downtown Hood River with his beautiful wife, Jan, son Nathaniel, and daughters Julia and Emma.

If You Go

▶ **Getting There:** Most visitors fly in to Portland; Hood River is sixty miles east.

▶ **Best Time to Visit:** Hood River offers four-season recreation. The most reliable wind/weather conditions for windsurfing/kiteboarding happen June through September, though many locals are on the water year-round. You needn't be experienced to try; several companies offer beginner lessons.

▶ **Spots to Visit:** Full Sail Brewing (541-386-2247; www.fullsailbrewing.com); Double Mountain Brewery (541-387-0042; www.doublemountainbrewery.com); Pfriem Family Brewers (541-321-0490; www.pfriembeer.com); Logsdon Farmhouse Ales (503-679-8063; www.farmhousebeer.com); Big Horse Brew Pub (541-386-4411; www.bighorsebrewpub.com). There are several fine brewers a short drive from Hood River on the Washington side, including Everybody's Brewing (509-637-2774; www.everybodysbrewing.com) and Walking Man Brewing (509-427-5520; www.walkingmanbeer.com). Visit www.breweries inthegorge.com for a full list.

▶ **Accommodations:** Hood River County Chamber of Commerce (800-366-3530; www.hoodriver.org) highlights places to stay in and near Hood River.

DESTINATION

40

PORTLAND

RECOMMENDED BY **John Foyston**

When making the case for Portland's spot as America's top beer city in a recent story on CNN, John Foyston let the numbers do the talking: "There are more than sixty brewing establishments in the city, including a dozen breweries and brewpubs within a few square blocks in the Southeast district. According to supermarket tracking services, Portland leads the United States in percentage of craft beer sales, with nearly forty percent of beer purchases being craft beer. And, the city is home to over one hunded beer festivals, including the Oregon Brewers Festival, which attracts more than eighty-five thousand people a year."

Portland rests at the confluence of the Columbia and Willamette Rivers, at the northern end of Oregon's Willamette Valley. For many years, Portland lived in the shadow of its flashier neighbors, San Francisco and Seattle, quietly walking its own walk. Recently the city's proximity to the coast and the mountains, its emerging "foodie" culture, and its progressive "green" aura have thrust it into the limelight. (You know you've arrived when a cable program satirizing your mores appears!) The beer certainly burnishes that special Portland aura, though it's nothing new; several of Portland's beer pioneers date back to 1984. John has seen it all. "In the early days, there were the McMenamins, the Widmers, Art Larrance and Fred Bowman at Portland Brewing, and Nancy and Dick Ponzi at BridgePort. They all made a huge difference. [Part of that difference was lobbying to change Oregon law so beer could be served on the premises where it was created, thus giving birth to brewpubs and tasting rooms.] Don Younger and his Horse Brass Pub also played an important role, as he was featuring craft beers on tap in the eighties, before it was popular. Horse Brass still lives on and is Portland's most famous pub, and though Don died in 2011, his spirit still informs the place."

Throw a rock in most Portland neighborhoods and you've got a decent chance of hitting a McMenamins, an empire of breweries and pubs (twenty-five or so in the city, with many more in surrounding communities) launched by the brothers Mike and Brian, circa 1985. The McMenamins brought Ruby Ale (a lighter raspberry-infused ale), Hammerhead (a coppery pale ale), and Terminator (a full-bodied stout); perhaps more importantly, they brought the City of Roses a passion for historic preservation, repurposing a number of forgotten and deteriorating buildings into thriving concerns that blend beer, food, and music and act as neighborhood anchors. (One favorite is Kennedy School, where overnight guests sleep in old classrooms, replete with chalk boards.) The Widmer Brothers—Kurt and Rob—brought Portland beer to a broader market through their popular American hefeweizen, an unfiltered wheat beer, and also were the first brewer to offer a full four-season beer lineup. BridgePort brewed the IPA (in 1994) that set the stage for the IPA craze that's still going strong, in Portland and beyond.

It would take a week (or three) to visit all of Portland's breweries, brewpubs, and taphouses. There's a pub decorated with custom frames from Portland bicycle makers (Hopworks BikeBar), a gluten-free brewery (Ground Breaker), and a nonprofit brewery (Ex Novo) that donates profits to good causes . . . and new models are always coming online. To get a further sense of where Portland's brewing scene came from and where it's going, John suggested a few key stops. "To understand the birth of the Portland brewpub, you need to visit the original Lucky Lab on Hawthorne. You could argue that BridgePort or the Hillsdale McMenamins were the first brewpubs here, but Lucky Lab incorporated all of the crotchets that we associate with brewpubs—the barely worked-over industrial space, the dog-a-rific back porch. It's still that way today."

Portland built much of its reputation on the hoppy shoulders of its IPAs, but hop-forward beers are by no means the only game in town. America's sour beer movement has roots here as well. "Ron Gansberg at Cascade Brewing Barrel House basically invented the sour beer category," John explained. "At one point, he decided he didn't want to join the IPA movement, though it wasn't for a lack of trying. Years back, at Cascade's other location, Raccoon Lodge, he went so far as to put an IPA into oak barrels, gently agitate them, and put them through temperature changes to simulate the voyage to India. He's incapable of doing anything normal, is a complete loon, and is creative as hell. If you like sour beers at all, you must visit the Barrel House. If you go on a Tuesday, they do a live barrel tapping at six P.M. They choose a couple people to tap the barrel with a spigot and hammer. This has led to the term 'Sour Shower,' which is the result when you have novice beer tappers. It's worth watching . . . from a distance.

"Alan Sprints's Hair of the Dog should also be on your list, for so many reasons. In a world where everybody wants to get huge and sell their beer everywhere, Alan just wants to make six hundred barrels a year, and he wants to brew it in a vessel that may or may not be an old Campbell's Soup kettle. His brewery is pretty much unchanged for twenty-one years. For many years, Hair of the Dog was in a heavily industrial area of Southeast Portland and pretty hard to find. Now the pub is much more accessible at the east end of the Morrison Bridge. He brews amazing beers, and is a fine chef too. Alan is a Portland treasure."

JOHN FOYSTON is Oregon's longest-serving beer writer and wrote a weekly beer column for the Oregonian for nearly twenty years. His work has appeared on CNN and in *Beer Connoisseur*, *Celebrator Beer News*, *Oregon Beer Growler*, *Mix Magazine*, and *Brewpublic*. In his spare time, John is a vintage Ducati motorcycle specialist and a fine artist. You can follow John on Twitter at @beerherejohnny.

If You Go

▶ **Getting There:** Portland is served by most major carriers.

▶ **Best Time to Visit:** You'll find the most reliable weather from June through mid-October, though various beer-oriented events are on tap throughout the year. The Oregon Brewers Festival (www.oregonbrewfest.com) is held the last weekend in July each year.

▶ **Spots to Visit:** Horse Brass Pub (503-232-2202; www.horsebrass.com); any McMenamins (www.mcmenamins.com); Lucky Lab on Hawthorne (503-236-3555; www.luckylab.com); Cascade Brewing Barrel House (503-265-8603; www.cascadebrewingbarrelhouse.com); Hair of the Dog (503-232-6585; www.hairofthedog.com); BeerMongers (503-234-6012; www.thebeermongers.com).

▶ **Accommodations:** Travel Portland (877-678-5263; www.travelportland.com) lists lodging options in the Rose City, as well as a number of beer-tour operators.

DESTINATION

41

PHILADELPHIA

RECOMMENDED BY **Don "Joe Sixpack" Russell**

Since the mid-aughts, Philadelphia has declared itself "America's Best Beer-Drinking City"—not to be confused with "America's Beer Capital," a distinction claimed by any number of burgs. Ruminating on the city's beer history, Don Russell shed light on the subtleties therein. "Philadelphia has had a vibrant tavern culture going back more than three hundred years, to colonial times. When Ben Franklin arrived here [from his birthplace in Boston], it's likely that one of his first stops was a tavern for a drink, something to eat, and a place to stay. Taverns were a focal point of life in Philadelphia in Franklin's time, and this tradition continues today. The city's thriving tavern culture is fueled by the fact that Philly is not a commuter town. People don't just work here, they live here. Go to any neighborhood—Center City, South Philly, the River Wards—you'll find people frequenting their neighborhood tavern. This long-standing tavern culture is really the backbone of Philadelphia's beer scene."

Records show that at the time of the Revolutionary War, Philadelphia (along with Boston) had a tavern for every twenty-five men—a greater concentration of drinking establishments than anywhere else in the British Empire. Beer and ale were the libations of choice. Pennsylvania was, of course, an English colony, but there was also a large influx of German immigrants. Both brought their brewing traditions. (An advertisement dating back to the 1850s for Engel and Wolf's brewery proclaims "The First Lager Beer Brewery in America.") By the late 1800s there were nearly two hundred breweries operating in Philadelphia and its immediate surroundings; one neighborhood in North Philly had some twenty breweries at its peak and was known as Brewerytown. (The neighborhood remains, though the large-scale breweries are long departed.) Prohibition gutted Philly's brewing culture; few of the breweries that were shuttered by the Eighteenth Amendment

OPPOSITE:
Philadelphia has
a rich tavern
culture going
back to colonial
times. McGillin's
Olde Ale House
is Philly's oldest
standing tavern,
dating to 1860.

DESTINATION

42

189

reopened their doors once it was repealed. The taverns reopened, of course, although with a less robust selection of suds. But tavern owners were ready when better alternatives were presented.

"The bars and taverns are very diverse and independent," Don continued. "Chains are not players in the beer scene here. A bar owner here might have at most two or three properties. Many are owned by bartenders who saved and eventually went out and bought their own places, or children who had the bar passed down from their parents. When craft brewing arrived, many publicans were willing to put the good beers on tap. First it was some of the imports from Belgium and England, then West Coast ales. When the local craft breweries started coming online, they were incorporated into the mix. Philadelphia also has a thriving food scene, and it's attached at the hip to beer. Taverns were always a place to go for a cheap and convenient dinner, even if you didn't drink. Taverns have attracted many promising chefs over the years. Some of the most prominent chefs in the city have their roots in corner bars. Now, chefs are pairing meals with beers instead of wine."

Greater Philadelphia has fifty-plus craft brewers operating, creating a variety of styles—from IPAs to saisons. The two breweries that set the tone in large part for the kinds of beers that are being made are Yards and Victory. "Yards brews British-style beers," Don said, "and is right in North Philly, on the Delaware River. Victory is in the suburb of Chester, and they focus more on German styles." Dock Street (in West Philly) and Stoudts (in suburban Adamstown) were also early players. "If there's one style that's distinctly Philadelphia, I'd have to say it's pilsner," Don added. "Doing a story ten years back, I realized that over a ten-year period, fifty percent of the pilsner medals awarded at the Great American Beer Festival were won by breweries within a forty-mile circle of Philadelphia. It's a difficult style to brew, but done right it's very light and approachable. Stoudts and Tröegs both make wonderful pilsners."

As far as Don Russell is concerned, you can get a good sense of Philly's beer scene popping into any corner bar, from South Philly to Fairmount. A few old favorites that stand out are McGillin's Old Ale House and Khyber Pass. "McGillin's is the city's oldest standing tavern, dating back to 1860. It's right in Center City and is the prototypical Philly bar, specializing in Pennsylvania beers. Khyber Pass is in the Old City section and is the city's second-oldest bar. It's one of the leading spots for high-end beers—not limited to locals—and has good food. A distinctly Philly experience can be had in the Mayfair neighborhood at the Grey Lodge. Each Friday the thirteenth, the pub celebrates Friday the Firkinteenth, loading up the bar with twenty to thirty cask-conditioned ales. People will drop in for breakfast and have a cask beer."

Don has been a newspaper reporter for nearly forty years in addition to being a beloved beer columnist. One of his most memorable investigative stories underscores the connection Philadelphians have with beer. "Back in 1998, I did a piece about the beer being poured at the old Veterans Stadium, home of the Philadelphia Phillies baseball team. I had received a tip that the company running the concessions [Ogden Entertainment] had been shorting people on their pours. Vendors had been told to pour beers with a healthy head, but the glasses were too small to hold the amount of beer advertised. Up to that point, I'd written hundreds of stories—big investigative pieces on political scandals and other major news items. But this story generated the most mail. People were outraged that the stadium was cheating them out of their beer. The city cracked down on the scandal, and the concessionaire lost their contract. By Opening Day 1999, there was a new concessionaire and a new beer policy was rolled out—prices were dropped, and bigger cups were introduced. I happened to be there on Opening Day when the new beer policy was announced over the public-address system. I was brought down to the field and given a standing ovation.

"The whole experience showed me that beer was something that Philadelphians cared about . . . and that when someone was going to try to steal this from us, we'd take it personally."

DON RUSSELL (aka Joe Sixpack) is an award-winning Philadelphia writer who's written about crooked pols, stupid criminals, and a flying pig. His reports led to the federal government's first-ever environmental racketeering prosecution, the closure of a county jail, the reform of the Philadelphia taxicab industry, numerous criminal indictments, and a highly publicized face-off with the Philadelphia Eagles that eventually ended the team's ban on football fans' infamous "Hoagies of Mass Destruction." Launched in the *Philadelphia Daily News* in 1996, Don's "Joe Sixpack" is one of Philadelphia's longest-running newspaper columns of any kind. He's the author of three books: *Joe Sixpack's Philly Beer Guide: A Reporter's Notes on the Best Beer-Drinking City in America* (Camino Books); *Christmas Beer: The Cheeriest, Tastiest, Most Unusual Holiday Brews* (Rizzoli Universe); and *What the Hell Am I Drinking?* (CreateSpace). Don has won numerous

DESTINATION

42

awards for his beer columns, including twenty Quill & Tankard trophies from the North American Guild of Beer Writers. In 2002 and 2006, he was named Beer Writer of the Year at the Great American Beer Festival. Don is a founder and original executive director of Philly Beer Week, a nonprofit organization promoting Philadelphia as "America's Best Beer-Drinking City." He lives in Philadelphia with his wife, Theresa Conroy, a certified yoga therapist and studio operator, and their Siberian Husky, Karma. Learn more about Don/Joe at www.joesixpack.net.

If You Go

▶ **Getting There:** Philadelphia is served by most major carriers.
▶ **Best Time to Visit:** Philly Beer Week occurs the first week of June each year, and has ten days of beer events with 150 to 200 bars participating. Time a visit to coincide with a Friday the 13th so you can take in a Firkinteenth tapping at the Grey Lodge.
▶ **Spots to Visit:** Yards Brewing Company (215-634-2600; www.yardsbrewing.com); Dock Street Brewery (215-726-2337; www.dockstreetbeer.com); Stoudts Brewing (717-484-4386; www.stoudts.com); McGillin's Olde Ale House (215-735-5562; www.mcgillins.com); Khyber Pass Pub (215-238-5888; www.khyberpasspub.com); the Grey Lodge (215-856-3591; www.greylodge.com).
▶ **Accommodations:** Visit Philadelphia (800-537-7676; www.visitphilly.com) is a good clearinghouse for lodging options.

DESTINATION

42

MONTREAL

RECOMMENDED BY **Marc-André Gauvreau**

Montreal is a city where old and new come together in surprising and pleasing ways. Here, Old World European charm happily coexists with the energy of a thriving youth culture, fueled by the city's many universities. Cutting-edge art and music coincide with quiet strolls on the cobblestoned lanes of Old Montreal. A decidedly French atmosphere embraces a melting pot of different cultures and ethnicities. And a craft beer movement thrives happily in the shadow of Canada's biggest and oldest brewer.

"For me, Montreal is close to a beer paradise," Marc-André Gauvreau began. "There are more than a hundred and twenty small breweries around this part of Quebec. The growth has been driven in part by the somewhat protectionist laws we have in Canada. In the U.S., you can have humongous central breweries in cities like Milwaukee and St. Louis and distribute your beer all over. In Canada, you have to have a physical brewery in a province to sell your product in that province. It would be easier for me to sell beer in Africa than in Toronto. What's brewed in Quebec stays in Quebec. In the States you have pure capitalism; in Canada, we have a form of democratic socialism."

Any talk of Canada and beer—especially Montreal and beer—must begin with Molson. John Molson emigrated to Montreal from England in 1782 and soon after found work at a local brewery owned by one Thomas Loyd. Molson showed a knack for brewing, but an even more astute sense of business. Seeing the potential for beer sales among other immigrants from England and Ireland, he arranged to purchase the brewery from Loyd. Recognizing the need for a steady supply of barley malt, he traveled to Europe and came back to Montreal with sacks of barley seeds, which he distributed to local farmers free of charge. Molson's first beers were delivered in 1786 and were well received. Thus, a dynasty was born. John Molson went on to invest in a number of other businesses while growing the brewery; his progeny continued to expand the empire, adding to the portfolio perhaps the most iconic Quebec brand—the Montreal Canadiens. Beer is still brewed at the site of the original brewery in Montreal, and Molson is the best-selling Canadian beer in Canada, though not the best-selling beer in Canada; that honor goes to Budweiser.

"Many of the younger kids who are brewing now, they see Molson as an atrocity," Marc-André continued. "They view Molson as big and mean and ugly. I have gray hair and a white beard, and I don't see it that way. Molson is the mothership. They helped establish the brewing industry in Canada, and for that, I'm thankful."

Montreal brewers have certainly moved beyond the golden ales that make up the foundation of Molson's offerings. "Right now, I'd say that many brewers are following trends set in the United States," Marc-André observed. "One year, it's beers matured in oak casks. The next, it's IPAs with IBU ratings over one hundred. But given our French origins, Belgian styles also have an influence on our brewing. Brewers are doing lambics and sour styles. I try to make beers that are a little more approachable, a little easier to drink. We [at Brasseur de Montréal] do a lot of session ales and fruit beers. One of our best sellers, Chi Orientale, is a witbier made with ginger and lemongrass; it's a perfect complement for delicate Asian foods. Sometimes the kids with tattoos look at me as an older guy who makes sissy beers that aren't alcoholized enough. Now and again I'll bring out something to kick their butt." One of these offerings is Ghosttown, an absinthe-based stout brewed with roots and herbs. "It's one of the most complex beers you'll ever taste," Marc-André added. "You love it or hate it."

Marc-André also shared a few of his favorite brewpubs around Montreal. "Dieu du Ciel! makes fantastic beer, and they always have a beer on one of the top–one hundred lists," he shared. "La Cheval Blanc is one of the oldest brewpubs in the city and focuses mostly on Belgian ale styles." He also likes L'Amère à Boire (which does both German- and British-style ales), Benelux (which brews styles ranging from Flemish reds to double IPAs), and Les Soeurs Grises (which tends toward Belgian ales). Perhaps the best way to get a flavor of Montreal's craft beer scene is to attend Mondial de la Bière, which is held in mid-June. "It attracts seventy-five thousand people over five days—a huge event," Marc-André enthused. "Though the beer is flowing freely, everyone is smiling. There are two or three fights at the most."

If there's a time and place that captures the spirit of enjoying a good beer in Montreal, it might be a spring or summer evening at Le Saint-Sulpice. "Le Saint-Sulpice is in the city's Latin Quarter, very walkable from Old Montreal and near Quebec University," Marc-André said. "It's a huge establishment—it must hold two thousand people. It has eleven or twelve bars and a terrace that holds four hundred. Once summer arrives, people go nuts. Saint-Sulpice will be a crowded place, but it can be crazy, fun times."

And as any good Montrealer who's enjoyed an extra beer now and again will tell you, the only way to end the evening is with a bowl of poutine (pronounced poo-TEEN), the curious (and rather caloric) plate of fries, cheese curds, and brown gravy. Once reserved for less-discriminating late-night diners, poutine has been embraced by the culinary establishment. You can now find double-pork peppercorn poutine, curry chicken poutine, or fois gras poutine, among many other inspirations.

MARC-ANDRÉ GAVREAU is a longtime beer lover. He started his career in 1985 working for a Montreal-based company that distributes Guinness. In 1991, he became one of the first keg market developer representatives for Unibroue in the Quebec Region. In 1996, he worked at Brasal for a few months before switching over to Les Brasseurs du Nord. A few years later, he was promoted to the regional sales manager position. In 2007, he and his spouse and partner, Denise Mérineau, founded Brasseur de Montréal.

If You Go

▶ **Getting There:** Montreal is served by most major carriers.

▶ **Best Time to Visit:** Festival Mondial de la Bière (514-722-9640; www.festivalmondial biere.qc.ca) is held in mid-June.

▶ **Spots to Visit:** Brasseur de Montréal (514-788-4505; www.brasseurdemontreal.com) Dieu du Ciel! (514-490-9555; www.dieuduciel.com); Le Cheval Blanc (514-522-0211; www. lechevalblanc.ca); L'Amère à Boire (514-282-7448; www.amereaboire.com) Benelux (514-543-9750; www.brasseriebenelux.com); Les Soeurs Grises (514-788-7635; www.bblsg. com); Le Saint-Sulpice (514-844-9458; www.lesaintsulpice.ca).

▶ **Accommodations:** Tourism Montreal (514-844-5400; www.tourisme-montreal.org) lists lodging options around the city.

DESTINATION

43

ST. ANDREWS

RECOMMENDED BY **Christopher Bittenbender**

Chris Bittenbender didn't come to St. Andrews for the beer. But it certainly made a great study aid.

"I'd first heard about St. Andrews when I was an English major at Middlebury College, considering taking a year abroad," he shared. "I did end up doing my junior year in Scotland, but at University of Stirling. I took a day trip to St. Andrews at one point and fell in love with the place. I thought at the time, 'If I ever go to graduate school, I'd love to go there.' At the time I was interested in studying Irish literature. One of my professors gave me *Lanark*, by Alasdair Gray, considered one of Scotland's great men of letters. Reading *Lanark* got me interested in Scottish literature. As I began considering graduate programs, St. Andrews jumped to the top of my list. I was fortunate enough to get in."

St. Andrews was founded between 1410 and 1413, making it the third-oldest university in Great Britain, behind only Oxford and Cambridge. It's also ranked as the United Kingdom's third-best university . . . behind Oxford and Cambridge. Today, St. Andrews has eight thousand students in attendance, including some one thousand graduate students. Students, of course, enjoy access to the university's various athletic grounds . . . including the golf courses that sit just north of campus.

One story regarding the birth of golf goes something like this: A group of shepherds watching over their flocks along the eastern coast of Scotland in the late 1400s or early 1500s became bored. Armed with the tools of their trade—namely crooks—and acting on the natural male instinct to hit things (in this case, pebbles, or, as some have suggested, dried sheep dung), the first informal match was played. The relatively barren, rugged turf of the coast proved well-suited for the pursuit of a pastime where controlling the direction

OPPOSITE:
Golfers from all corners of the world make the pilgrimage to the Old Course at St. Andrews, the world's oldest and most famous golf course. Several great "nineteenth holes" wait after the round.

DESTINATION

44

197

of a small projectile could be challenging. It's believed that a favorite gathering place of these very early linksters was the turf that would one day become the Old Course.

Now, some five hundred years later, nearly every soul who's picked up a club and been smitten by the game dreams of one day making "The Pilgrimage" to have his or her picture snapped on the Swilcan Bridge, with the venerable Royal and Ancient Clubhouse looming in the background. "Most things that are five hundred years old are resting under glass in a museum," writer John Barton has posited. "This course is still alive, and you walk in the footsteps of five centuries of players." Despite its absolute and indelible association with the game of golf, the Old Course is something of a surprise for some Americans. It doesn't look much like an American's vision of a course, much less a vision of one of the greatest courses in the world. There are no trees, and the topography viewed from afar seems mundanely flat; in the 1820s, the course narrowly escaped becoming a rabbit farm. Sam Snead, in passing the Old Course by train en route to the British Open in 1946, remarked, "That looks like an old abandoned golf course." This slight aside, Snead went on to win the championship.

The students of St. Andrews and the golfers of St. Andrews may not always agree on theories of literary criticism or approach shots, but they can concur on the pleasures of a good pint at the end of the day. While Scotland's bigger, less adventurous brands—Tennent's Lager and McEwan's—are still present in many pubs, there are many more real ales (that is, ales drawn from a cask) available. They tend toward a lower ABV and a subdued hop profile. (Historically, hops were not always available in Scotland, as they couldn't be grown here.) Like everywhere else, more craft brewers are popping up and embracing more diverse styles.

One spot that's favored by university students is the Cellar Bar, which features an average of nine real ales each week. (The Cellar is proud of being featured in the Campaign for Real Ales' Good Beer Guide for twenty-five years running and is also considered one of St. Andrews's premiere live music venues.) "A little closer to the Royal and Ancient Golf Club (R&A), you'll find Ma Bells," Chris continued. "It's in the Hotel du Vin on the Scores, which is the road that runs from the R&A to the St. Andrews Castle. When the British Open is held here, you'll see a lot of famous players around Ma Bells."

A must-stop for visiting golfers is the Jigger Inn, now connected to the Old Course Hotel. "The Jigger dates back to the 1800s and basically adjoins the Road Hole (seventeenth hole) on the Old Course," Chris explained. "If you're a good player, you try to aim your tee shot over the corner of the Old Course Hotel to shorten your approach shot." The Jigger has ample golf memorabilia, some good views of the seventeenth hole, and all the tartan and dark wood paneling one might expect from a pub on the edge of the world's oldest golf course. It serves up, among other Scottish ales, Jigger Ale, made by Belhaven, Scotland's oldest independent brewery.

There's no doubt that St. Andrews's most elusive beer is served at the Royal and Ancient Golf Club, the iconic edifice that rests behind the eighteenth green at the Old Course. "On one occasion, I got as far as the hallway," Chris recalled. "But I wasn't able to get anywhere near the bar." To enjoy that privilege, you'll need an invitation into the club-house from a member.

J. CHRISTOPHER BITTENBENDER, PHD, is the co-chair of the English Department at Eastern University in Philadelphia and also teaches courses on British, Scottish, and American literature. He lives in Philadelphia with his son and daughter. While his golf game has suffered since leaving St. Andrews, he can sometimes be found enjoying a pint at Race Street Café (www.racestreetcafe.net).

If You Go

▶ **Getting There:** St. Andrews is roughly 1.5 hours from Edinburgh and two hours from Glasgow, both served by many major carriers.

▶ **Best Time to Visit:** Summer and fall hold the best hope for dry weather, though conditions change very rapidly. The Old Course is frequently closed in winter months for maintenance; tee times can be reserved in advance, though the course is very busy in the summer. Visit St. Andrews Links (www.standrews.com) for details.

▶ **Spots to Visit:** Cellar Bar (+44 1334 477425; www.cellarbar.co.uk); Ma Bells (+44 1334 472611; www.hotelduvin.com/locations/st-andrews/ma-bells); Jigger Inn (+44 1334 474371; www.oldcoursehotel.co.uk).

▶ **Accommodations:** An overview of possible accommodations can be found at Visit St. Andrews (+44 1334 472021; www.visitstandrews.com).

AUSTIN

RECOMMENDED BY **Mark Floreani**

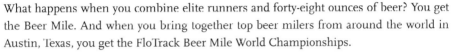

What happens when you combine elite runners and forty-eight ounces of beer? You get the Beer Mile. And when you bring together top beer milers from around the world in Austin, Texas, you get the FloTrack Beer Mile World Championships.

"The Beer Mile has always had an underground appeal for runners," Mark Floreani began. "For some, it's a rite of passage. With the World Championships, we wanted to bring the Beer Mile to the forefront, with a formal competition and world champions. It's a great intersection between the running world and popular culture."

While there's some suggestion that runners had experimented with variations of the beer mile concept in the early eighties, *Runner's World* traces its genesis to a track in Burlington, Ontario, on an August night in 1989. Seven young running friends (including Graham Hood, who would later run the 1,500 meters in the Olympics) had concocted a plan—drink four beers, sprint four laps, beer, lap, beer, lap, etc. The runners lined up four unopened cans of beer for themselves at the starting line, the timer was started, and the race began. The runners guessed that the beer would pose challenges, but those challenges were not what they'd expected; the alcohol wasn't a problem as much as the carbonation, which creates a tangible level of discomfort. Happy with their experiment, some of the original runners carried the contest along with them to Queen's University in Kingston, Ontario, T-shirts were made, and the Beer Mile became a part—albeit a small part—of the track-and-field canon.

As the Beer Mile has come out of the shadows, a codified set of rules has emerged:

1. Each competitor drinks four cans of beer and runs four laps, ideally on a track (start—beer, then lap, then beer, then lap, then beer, then lap—finish).
2. Beer must be consumed before the lap is begun, within the transition area, which is

OPPOSITE:
Beer Mile
participants must
down four twelve-
ounce cans/bottles
of beer—one for
each quarter
mile—and keep
everything down.

DESTINATION

45

the 10-meter zone before the start/finish line on a 400-meter track.

3. The race begins with the drinking of the first beer in the last meter of the transition zone to ensure the competitors run a complete mile (1609 meters).

4. Women also drink four beers in four laps.

5. Competitors must drink canned beer and the cans should not be less than 355ml (the standard can volume) or 12 oz (the imperial equivalent). Bottles may be substituted for cans as long as they are at least 12 oz (355 ml) in volume.

6. No specialized cans or bottles may be used that give an advantage by allowing the beer to pour at a faster rate.

7. Beer cans must not be tampered with in any manner, ie. no shotgunning or puncturing of the can except for opening the can by the tab at the top. The same applies with bottles—no straws or other aids are allowed in order to aid in the speed of pouring.

8. Beer must be a minimum of 5 percent alcohol by volume. Hard ciders and lemonades will not suffice. The beer must be a fermented alcoholic beverage brewed from malted cereal grains and flavored with hops.

9. Each beer can must not be opened until the competitor enters the transition zone on each lap.

10. Competitors who evacuate any beer before they finish the race must complete one penalty lap at the end of the race (immediately after the completion of their fourth lap). Note: Vomiting more than once during the race still requires only one penalty lap at the end. It is strongly recommended, when attempting official records, to tip the empty beer can or bottle over your head at the end of a chug to verify an empty vessel.

Competitors at the Beer Mile World Championships draw from a spectrum of runners/beer drinkers. Participants range from Olympians and top-ranked beer milers to far less serious runners with a thirst for adventure; in 2014, an eighty-year-old woman participated in the race. Winners receive a cash prize of $2,500. "The key to success is the ability to drink beer fast," Mark continued. "Six to twelve seconds is the preferred range. Corey Gallagher, 2014's champion, did a five-minute mile that consisted of thirty-eight seconds of drinking beer and four minutes and twenty-two seconds of running. He chugged his last beer in 6.7 seconds. In 2014, professional athletes didn't tend to do as well as serious amateurs who had mastered the beer drinking." Not surprisingly, lagers on the lighter side of the scale tend to be favored by beer milers. According to statistics compiled on beermile.com, the five most popular products are Budweiser, Pabst Blue Ribbon, Miller

High Life, Coors, and Heineken. Gallagher's beer of choice for his winning run was Bud Ice. The female champion in 2014, a forty-five-year-old mother of six named Chris Kimbrough, favored an altbier called Alt-eration from local brewer Hops & Grain.

You needn't be among the over two hundred participants to enjoy the Beer Mile World Championships. The race site (this year, the grounds of the Austin American-Statesman) is open to the public and features food trucks, live music—and for those attendees who'd like the opportunity to enjoy a more leisurely beer—a beer garden. The 2015 beer garden featured KCCO Gold Lager, made by theCHIVE, an Austin-based entertainment website. KCCO stands for "Keep Calm and Chive On." (The Beer Mile World Championships are also streamed live at the FloTrack website.)

Should you have room for another brew after completing the race, Austin won't disappoint. There are more than thirty breweries and brewpubs operating in the city. If you enjoy Austin-style country music, you'll want to hunt down at least one Robert Earl Keen Honey Pils, a collaborative project between Pedernales Brewing in the hill country west of town and one of Texas's most beloved Americana singer-songwriters.

MARK FLOREANI is the cofounder and COO of FloSports, which administers FloTrack, a website dedicated to coverage of track and field, and hosts the Beer Mile World Championships.

If You Go

▶ **Getting There:** Austin is served by most major carriers.

▶ **Best Time to Visit:** The FloTrack Beer Mile World Championships are held in early December.

▶ **Spots to Visit:** The Flo Track website (www.flotrack.org) will list the exact location of future World Beer Championship events. The South Congress district has a great assemblage of watering holes for a post-race beer. Locals say that on a hot summer's day, it's hard to beat a Lone Star at Barton Springs.

▶ **Accommodations:** Austin Visitors & Convention Bureau (512-474-5171; www.austin texas.org) lists lodging options around the "Live Music Capital of the World."

DESTINATION

45

MOAB

RECOMMENDED BY **Russ Facente**

The town of Moab sits between Arches and Canyonlands National Parks, among a remarkable patchwork of canyons, mesas, and deep river gorges. It's easy to enjoy the thousands of square miles of red rock vistas from the seat of your car . . . though thousands come each year to enjoy them from the seat of a mountain bike.

OPPOSITE:
Mountain bikers
flock to Moab
for trails like

"Moab is the kind of destination where anyone who likes the outdoors will find something to do," began Russ Facente. "There's skydiving, riding ATVs, white-water rafting, rock climbing—and, most notably, mountain biking. You'll find some of the most technical terrain anywhere around Moab. People come from around the world to ride one-of-a-kind trails like Slickrock. Eight years ago, there wasn't quite as much for less-seasoned riders. But many new trails have been added, especially at Dead Horse Point State Park."

the Magnificent
Seven. And
though this is
Utah, locally
brewed beer
awaits after

And you can rest assured that, although this is Utah, a cold beer will be waiting at the end of the day.

the ride.

Most trace the roots of modern mountain biking to Marin County, California, in the early seventies, though a case could be made that people have been going off road since the bicycle was created. Armed with old single-speed bikes outfitted with balloon tires, a handful of Marin teenagers (known as the Larkspur Canyon Gang) attacked Mount Tamalpais above Mill Valley. Other road bikers soon followed suit, and not long after, the first race was organized—Repack—so named because riders would have to repack their brakes with grease after each race, thanks to the braking the steep descent demanded. Hence a new sport was born . . . though it wouldn't be called mountain biking until 1979. Enthusiasts recognized the potential of Moab and its geologic wonders as a biking hub a few years later, though it really came on the scene in 1986 with the first Canyonlands Fat Tire Festival. As more riders began to make their way to Moab, the existing trail infrastructure began to seem inadequate. The community came together to garner resources to expand the region's single-track system; the result was one hundred new miles of trails, cementing Moab's reputation as one of the world's foremost mountain biking destinations.

Now beer—or for that matter, any alcohol—has a somewhat ambiguous history in Utah. Contrary to popular beliefs, alcohol was not always strictly prohibited. Early Mormon settlers in the Salt Lake Valley built breweries as well as temples and recognized the commercial potential of producing and selling beer, wine, and even whiskey to non-believers passing through. It wasn't until Prohibition that abstinence was made Latter-Day Saints doctrine. Despite the fact that Mormons still make up the majority of Utah's population, an influx of newcomers drawn by the state's outdoor attractions coupled with the exigencies of a tourist economy have spawned some twenty brewing concerns in the Beehive State, including one in Moab. "The Moab Brewery is the only microbrewery in town," Russ continued. "They usually have eight or ten beers on draft, everything from a light pilsner to an oatmeal stout. By law, everything on draft is 3.2 percent alcohol by weight, though by volume, it's actually four percent. It's my understanding that Utah brewers make their beer to the four percent ABV, and that out-of-state producers that export into Utah brew their beer to full strength and then water it down, so it's better to 'go local' for the best flavor. Eddie McStiff's, a restaurant in town, has a number of beers on tap and the widest selection of bottled beer in town. While draft beer is only available in lower-alcohol-content forms, bottled and canned beer is available in standard-alcohol-content forms, though only in certain establishments . . . in Utah, it's a little hard to get used to the liquor laws."

As mentioned above, Moab has trails to suit riders with a range of skill levels. Russ shared a few of his recommendations. "Beginners will find lots of terrain at Dead Horse Point State Park as well as over at Moab Brands. For intermediate riders, I like the Klondike Bluffs area and Magnificent 7. The trails here add enough rocks to keep you on your toes, but not enough to have you fearing for your life if you're a less-seasoned rider. For advanced riders, Slickrock is a must." Slickrock is among the world's most famous mountain bike trails. The ten-plus-mile trail twists, climbs, turns, and descends on Navajo Sandstone, the geologic formation that accounts for many of the region's iconic rock attractions. Along the way, Slickrock offers up some tremendous Colorado River vistas. For riders seeking a multiday adventure, there's the White Rim Trail, which runs one hundred spectacular miles through Canyonlands National Park.

DESTINATION

46

In Moab, a beer always tastes best after a long day of riding. "There are a couple of rides that start up in the mountains," Russ described. "You can either get a shuttle up or do a self-shuttle where you leave one car at the end of the trail and take your buddy's car to the top. After a long ride, your body is craving water and salt. When you get to the bottom, it's great to have a cooler with some cold beer waiting. If you're a skilled rider, the Whole Enchilada [which combines six trails—Geyser Pass, Burro Pass, Hazzard County, part of Kokopelli, Upper and Lower Porcupine Singletrack, and Porcupine Rim—has 8,200 feet of downhill and 1,700 feet of climbing] might be the best experience. We get the same people coming in year after year to ride it; it's not one to miss. At the end of the thirty-mile ride, you descend to the Colorado River, where you can sit and soak it all in. I'm a stout guy, and my beer of choice would be an Old Rasputin Imperial Stout [from California's North Coast Brewing]. Though as that's a fairly strong [9 percent ABV] beer, I think I might eat something with it!"

RUSS FACENTE has been been enjoying bicycling since childhood, but really began riding hard after moving to Moab. He is assistant sales manager at Poison Spider Bicycles, which has been consistently rated one of America's best bike shops.

If You Go

▶ **Getting There:** The closest commercial airports to Moab are in Grand Junction, which is served by most major carriers; Grand Junction is served by several carriers, including American Airlines (800-433-7300; www.aa.com) and United (800-864-8331; www.united.com).

▶ **Best Time to Visit:** You'll find the mildest weather in spring and fall.

▶ **Spots to Visit:** The Moab Brewery (435-259-6333; www.themoabbrewery.com); Eddie McStiff's (435-259-2337; www.eddiemcstiffs.com); and Poison Spider Bicycles (800-635-1792; www.poisonspiderbicycles.com), for cycling guidance.

▶ **Accommodations:** The Moab Area Travel Council website (www.discovermoab.com) lists lodging options around Moab.

DESTINATION

46

GREATER BURLINGTON

RECOMMENDED BY **Matt Canning**

Matt Canning may have the best hotel job a beer lover could ever hope for: the role of beer concierge. "In 2013, I started working in the front office of the Hotel Vermont in Burlington," he recalled. "We would get a lot of questions about the local beer scene, and I was the go-to person. After a year of answering many of the same questions, the position of beer concierge was carved out. Not only do I field questions, but I get to lead a weekly all-day tour of some of my favorite breweries and pubs."

Perched between Lake Champlain, bucolic dairy farms, and the ski slopes of nearby Stowe, the small city of Burlington has always had a certain charm. In the last few decades, a world-class food and beer scene has emerged that's producing some of the most sought-after ales in North America, including Heady Topper. "In some places where there's a beer boom, being a local brewery is enough to make it on the local pub or restaurant's tap line," Matt explained. "But around Burlington, being local is not enough. People have high expectations about what they're going to serve, and you have to be good."

For fans of hop-forward beers, a chance to snatch up a can of Heady Topper double IPA may be reason enough to make the trek north to the Green Mountain State. Heady Topper has been brewed by the Alchemist, a family-run brewery in the town of Waterbury, since 2003. "This double IPA is not intended to be the strongest or most bitter DIPA," the Alchemist website proclaims. "But it is brewed to give you wave after wave of hop flavor without any astringent bitterness." Matt has described Heady Topper as having the big flavor and aroma of tropical fruit with a touch of pine . . . a chewy fruitiness without a bitter finish. (The beer is a result of a secret blend of six hops.) Heady Topper's flavor has inspired a cult following among Vermont hopheads, but a good deal of its allure stems from the challenge of finding it. For many years, it was only served at the Alchemist brew-

OPPOSITE:
To enjoy Hill Farmstead's beer, you pretty much have to travel to the brewery in Vermont's Northeast Kingdom.

pub. In 2011, a fifteen-barrel brewery and canning line was built; timing was propitious for Heady Topper fans, as the original brewpub was destroyed by Hurricane Irene two days before the first cans rolled off the line . . . and only the recipe for Heady Topper remained. Competition for the 180 barrels produced each week can be fierce.

"Many of our more celebrated beers (including Second Fiddle double IPA from Fiddlehead and Lawson's Sip of Sunshine) have extremely limited distribution," Matt continued, "and Heady Topper is a great example. So much of what I do in my role as beer concierge is directing people to where they can buy Heady Topper. There are a few shops in Burlington and the surrounding communities that retail the ale, and it's delivered to different stores on different days of the week. To get your four-pack of sixteen-ounce cans at some locations, you need to show up early at the store to get a ticket. Then you come back once the beer has been delivered to make your purchase. Local people trying to buy a sandwich or a cup of coffee can get fed up with the lines of customers waiting to buy beer. One local liquor store will answer the phone by telling callers that they have or don't have Heady Topper; that's how strong demand is."

The Alchemist Brewery is not open to the public, but some of greater Burlington's other notable breweries are. Matt shared a few of his favorite stops from his weekly tour. At the top of the list is Hill Farmstead. "If you want to take away some Hill Farmstead beer, you pretty much have to drive up to the Northeast Kingdom with your growlers, as they don't retail beer outside of the brewery," Matt described. [Some Hill Farmstead product is available in Vermont pubs.] "It's about an hour and forty-five minutes, but a very scenic drive through iconic Vermont countryside. After meandering through backroads, you reach a dirt road flanked by stone walls, and suddenly you're there—maybe not the setting you'd expect for one of the world's greatest breweries! Everything they brew is made with their own well water and is very memorable. Shaun Hill is usually there when we visit, but he's very focused on one thing—making great beer.

"My next stop is usually Lost Nation in the small town of Morrisville. Lost Nation focuses on session beers, which are yeast-driven and all under 5.5 percent ABV. Their philosophy is that their clientele lives in a rural area and have to drive longer distances, so make the beer with lower ABV without compromising taste. One of the owners, Allen Van Anda, is on hand to give a full tour. They have a beautiful outdoor beer garden and lots of hospitality. From here, we'll head south on Route 100, into Stowe. There are a few options here. If you want to try European-style lagers, stop at the Trapp brewery at the

Trapp Family Lodge. The brewery is mid-mountain and looks out over the valley and village of Stowe. If you're seeking a good IPA, stop at Idletyme and try the Doubletyme Double IPA. On the way back to Burlington, we'll stop in Waterbury. There are several great beer bars here—Prohibition Pig, Blackback Pub, and the Reservoir. You can find most of the region's great beers on tap here, sometimes even Heady Topper. On one of my tours, we found it at Prohibition and one of my guests cried."

MATT CANNING is the Beer Concierge at Hotel Vermont. A native of Burlington, VT. Matt has spent his life in the rich beer cultures of his hometown, the front range of Colorado and northern California. As the Beer Concierge, Matt acts as a resource for his guests traveling on beer tourism, this takes the form of beer tours to Vermont's most sought after breweries, tastings, educational sessions and information on where and when to find elusive beers. Matt loves drinking world class beer as a function of his job but the relationships that cultivate from enjoying beer with others is what he celebrates most. What is the favorite beer of a man who drinks beer for a living? His next beer.

If You Go

▶ **Getting There:** Burlington is served by many major carriers.

▶ **Best Time to Visit:** Many love to visit Vermont in the early fall, prime "leaf-peeping" time . . . but late spring and summers can be glorious.

▶ **Spots to Visit:** Hill Farmstead Brewery (802-533-7450; www.hillfarmstead.com); Lost Nation Brewing (802-851-8041; www.lostnationbrewing.com); Von Trapp Brewing (800-826-7000; www.vontrappbrewing.com); Idletyme (802-253-4765; www.idletymebrewing.com); Prohibition Pig (802-244-4120; www.prohibitionpig.com); the Blackback Pub (802-244-0123; www.theblackbackpub.com); the Reservoir (802-244-7827; www.waterburyreservoir.com).

▶ **Accommodations:** Hotel Vermont (855-650-0080; www.hotelvt.com) offers Matt's beer-concierge services. Lake Champlain Regional Chamber of Commerce (877-686-5253; www.vermont.org) highlights other lodging options.

DESTINATION

47

SEATTLE

RECOMMENDED BY **Nick Crandall**

In 1981, Kurt Cobain was fourteen years old and several years away from moving to Seattle; Microsoft had just been restructured and reincorporated in the state of Washington, with Bill Gates named president and chairman of the board; and Seattle beer drinkers looking for local suds mostly relied on Rainier and Olympia, light lagers that did little to challenge Emerald City taste buds.

But things began to change in 1982, when Redhook released its first ale from an old transmission shop in the Ballard neighborhood of Seattle, then still largely a town driven by the fortunes of Boeing. Their creation story is the stuff of legend in Washington brewing circles. A man with a bit of experience in the brewing realm—Gordon Bowker, who helped found Starbucks—joined forces with a marketing whiz named Paul Shipman with the goal of making a more flavorful beer . . . though neither had ever made beer themselves. Foregoing conventional wisdom, the duo—and their new brewmaster, Charles McEveley—passed on contracting their brewing out and instead cleaned up the transmission shop, purchased a used brew house from Germany, and set to work. The first batch, which was poured for an expectant crowd at a local tavern, had a slightly off, banana-like flavor. But it was unique enough to buy time for McEveley to create new flavors that would find a broader audience.

"For the first few years, Paul and Gordon were trying to explain to the public what it was they were brewing," Nick Crandall explained. "When many people thought of beer they thought of lagers that had been stripped of flavor during brewery consolidations. Redhook was educating people about traditional beer styles. It was a challenge to get people to buy in. They had to explain why a beer like Redhook cost more and why it was worth paying more."

OPPOSITE: Redhook put Seattle on America's beer map, and beer bars like Pine Box Tavern keep the flavorful suds flowing.

DESTINATION

48

The folks at Redhook laid the groundwork and were joined soon after by Hale's Ales (1983) and Pike Place Brewery (1989). With the combination of long, rainy winters (to send its citizens shuffling toward cozy pubs) and a constant flow of creative young people (both to make and drink craft beer), the Seattle beer scene burgeoned.

Redhook has undergone a number of changes over the years. It was the first craft brewery to be acquired (at least in part) by one of the conglomerate brewers. It was the first of West Coast craft brewers to open an East Coast operation (in Portsmouth, New Hampshire). And some years ago, it decamped from Seattle proper for its campus in the suburb of Woodinville, twenty minutes east (without traffic). But a spirit of adventure continues. "Redhook is always up to new stuff," Nick continued. "We recently rereleased a version of our double black stout that was originally made in the mid-nineties. At that time, we used Starbucks coffee. This time, we moved to a smaller coffee company, Caffe Vita. Redhook is the largest brewery in Washington, and that has a little bit of a downside in terms of our experimentation. If we create a new beer, we have to be able to go through one hundred full barrels." Redhook's Woodinville brewery has a bucolic setting that's adjacent to a bike trail that heads west into the city, making the brewery's Forecasters Pub on premises a popular weekend destination. The opening of a new Redhook pub in Capitol Hill in the fall of 2016 will help move Nick's newer creations.

Though Seattle may have lost some brewing mojo to its neighbor to the south and upstarts like Asheville, North Carolina, and Burlington, Vermont, there are many good things going on in the shadow of Mount Rainier. (Forty breweries can't be wrong!) "There are a number of spots that I'm excited about," Nick enthused. "Holy Mountain is new in the last year and is doing some cool barrel-aged beers with interesting yeasts. Black Raven (in Redmond) has consistently been brewing some of the area's best beer for the last six years. Fremont Brewing makes awesome pale ales as well as IPAs. [Fremont's Cowiche Canyon Organic Fresh Hop Ale, available after the hop harvest in early fall, is a special treat for pale ale fans.] Reuben's, in the nearby Ballard neighborhood, is also doing well. In terms of beer styles, this is still IPA country. There are a handful of brewpubs and taprooms that have tried opening without an IPA. All they hear the first few weeks is, 'Where's your IPA?' They might fight it for a while, but within six months, they're making an IPA. Hop-forward lagers are a trend I'm seeing— Holy Mountain, Black Raven, and Fremont all have offerings in this category. Session beers are also gaining momentum.

All the breweries above have taprooms featuring their wares. If you want to sample a variety of Seattle's finest ales without moving too far, Nick shared a few of his favorite beer bars. "Naked City, up in the north part of town, has a great vibe. They'll have roughly fifteen of their own beers on tap at a given time, and they'll have another twenty or so from other breweries flowing. Closer to downtown in South Lake Union, there's the Brave Horse Tavern, which has an amazing tap list and solid food. The Pine Box on Capitol Hill is where all the cool kids hang out, and they pay great attention to the beer list. My personal favorite—in part because of its proximity to my home in northeast Seattle—is the Beer Authority. It started out as a straight bottle shop, with something like four hundred labels. Then they added tastings. Then they put draft beer on. Now it's turned into a beer bar."

NICK CRANDALL is innovation brewer at Redhook. He got his start in the brewing world in Bellingham as a part-time keg washer at Boundary Bay Brewing while attending Western Washington University. Nick's time at Boundary Bay evolved into an intoxicating career that's included a stint at North Corner Brewing Supply and several positions at Redhook since joining the company in 2011.

If You Go

▶ **Getting There:** Seattle is served by most major carriers.
▶ **Best Time to Visit:** Seattle Beer Week (www.seattlebeerweek.com) is held in mid-May.
▶ **Spots to Visit:** Redhook Brewery (425-483-3232; www.redhook.com); Holy Mountain Brewing (www.holymountainbrewing.com); Black Raven Brewing (425-881-3020; www.blackravenbrewing.com); Fremont Brewing (206-420-2407; www.fremontbrewing.com); Reuben's Brews (206-784-2859; www.reubensbrews.com); Naked City Brewing (206-838-6299; www.nakedcitybrewing.com); Brave Horse Tavern (206-971-0717; www.bravehorsetavern.com); the Pine Box (206-588-0375; www.pineboxbar.com); Beer Authority (206-417-9629; www.seattlebeerauthority.com).
▶ **Accommodations:** Visit Seattle (866-732-2695; www.visitseattle.org) lists lodging options around the city; some deep discounts are available in the winter months.

DESTINATION

48

MILWAUKEE

RECOMMENDED BY **Dan Murphy**

The city of Milwaukee was once home to four of the world's largest brewers   Pabst, Schlitz, Miller, and Blatz. BeerHistory.com identifies several factors that helped the moderately sized city (current population less than six hundred thousand) to punch beyond its weight class as a beer powerhouse in its formative years. First, there was easy access to ice from the lake. In pre-refrigeration days, this both abetted the brewing process and facilitated shipping of fresh product. The proximity of a very thirsty megalopolis to the south also helped Milwaukee's brewer's flourish. The lake provided cheap and easy transportation to the Chicago market; sales skyrocketed after the Great Chicago Fire of 1871. Perhaps Milwaukee brewers' greatest accomplishment was determining a distribution chain that would allow their product to be shipped far and wide.

OPPOSITE: Milwaukee's big four made the city's beer reputation a reputation that's being burnished today by craft brewers like Lakefront.

But in the 1950s, the scene began to change. First, Blatz ("Milwaukee's Finest Beer") was sold to Pabst in 1958. Then Schlitz ("The Beer That Made Milwaukee Famous") was sold to Detroit-based Stroh's in 1982 (and then sold again in 1999, this time to Pabst). By 1996, Pabst ended beer production in Milwaukee and has bounced among various owners since, with current headquarters in Los Angeles . . . and a devoted following among twentysomething hipsters everywhere. Only Miller continues to maintain headquarters in Milwaukee . . . though with the acquisition by Anheuser-Busch InBev, how much longer they will stay is unclear.

Nonetheless, Milwaukee remains a great beer town, with new reinforcements rising to fill the void. "Milwaukee is a blue-collar town at heart, and I think the beer culture goes along with that," Dan Murphy observed. "There are still corner bars everywhere, a remnant of the old beer dynasties and the blue-collar ethos. These bars offer an outlet for the beer culture to continue, whatever beer is flowing. In the mid-eighties, as the older breweries were leaving and consolidating, new brewers started popping up, like Sprecher and Lakefront. This was before there were a lot of smaller breweries around; they were ahead of their time. People were drinking craft beer in Milwaukee before they realized they were drinking craft beer. It wasn't thought of that way; you'd see it at the local tavern, alongside Pabst and Miller. Though it should be noted that a lot of people wouldn't drink PBR after Pabst pulled out."

After almost thirty years in business, Lakefront and Sprecher are still going strong. Lakefront (established in 1987) sits above the Milwaukee River (though the lake is only a few blocks away), in the former location of the Milwaukee Electric Railway and Light Company's coal-fired power plant; they acquired the building, which was slated for demolition, after outgrowing the former bakery building where they'd started. Lakefront has proven innovative in many ways. The brothers Klisch, Jim and Russ, were the first to brew a 100 percent organic beer, the first to brew a 100 percent gluten-free beer, and the first since Prohibition to brew beer made with all-Wisconsin ingredients.

Milwaukee has strong German roots, and the beers that Sprecher produces reflect this tradition. "Their Black Bavarian [a dark Kulmbacher-style lager] gets very high marks," Dan said, "and they also make outstanding soda." Both Lakefront and Sprecher offer excellent brewery tours that have been embraced by many Milwaukee visitors as part of experiencing the "city that beer built." "One of the most interesting historic beer spots to visit is the old Pabst Brewery," Dan added. "It was this cool Gothic area rotting on the western edge of downtown, but now the whole neighborhood is getting revitalized. On the tour, the old executive bar room is a highlight." (Pabst, by the way, does have plans to resume limited brewing at one of its historic Milwaukee brewing sites.)

Considering Milwaukee's beer pedigree and corner-bar infrastructure, it's not surprising that the city boasts several celebrated taphouses. "The Bay View neighborhood has developed into a beer mecca, purely by happenstance," Dan continued. "There are three places within one and a half miles of each other that are all listed in *DRAFT* magazine's top one hundred beer bars—Romans' Pub, Palm Tavern, and Sugar Maple. If you could only visit one, it would have to be Romans'—not just for the beer list [which features over thirty American craft beers], but for the owner, Mike Romans. He's this barrel-chested, gruff guy who's loud and opinionated, but deep-down a good man. He took the big guys off draft before anyone else and will host events where he'll bring out stuff from his cellar. If you're a beer guy, you can talk to him for hours." Just down the street, Sugar Maple boasts sixty beers on tap; Palm Tavern offers twenty taps.

"Another beer bar that I really like that doesn't get the press it deserves is Burnhearts," Dan added. "It's a corner bar with great bartenders and a hipster vibe. Burnhearts hosts one of Milwaukee's best beer festivals, Mitten Fest. It's held in February. They have a stage set up outside with some of Milwaukee's best bands, and they bring out unique beers that are hard to find anywhere else, including barrel-aged beers from Central Waters, a brewery up north. Funds, clothing, and food are collected for the Hunger Task Force of Milwaukee."

If drinking beer in sub-freezing conditions is not your thing, you can attend a Brewers game. "Even with a bad season, Miller Park is a destination spot," Dan said. "The tailgating scene is amazing. For Friday night games, the lot is filled by five P.M., enveloped by the haze of hundreds of smoking grills."

DAN MURPHY is a fan of Milwaukee's beer and bar scene and has been writing about it for *Milwaukee Magazine* for more than a decade.

If You Go

▶ **Getting There:** Milwaukee is served by most major carriers.

▶ **Best Time to Visit:** Mitten Fest is generally held the first week of February. Those preferring milder temperatures will appreciate the many festivals held throughout the summer. The Wisconsin Craft Beer Festival is held in late October.

▶ **Spots to Visit:** Lakefront Brewery (414-372-8800; www.lakefrontbrewery.com); Sprecher (414-964-2739; www.sprecherbrewery.com; Best Place at the Historic Pabst Brewery (414-779-1663; www.bestplacemilwaukee.com); Romans' Pub (414-481-3396; www.romanspub.com); Sugar Maple (414-481-2393; www.mysugarmaple.com); Burnhearts (414-294-0490; www.burnheartsbar.com).

▶ **Accommodations:** Visit Milwaukee (800-554-1448; www.visitmilwaukee.org) lists lodging options around the city.

MANA POOLS NATIONAL PARK

RECOMMENDED BY **Tendai Mdluli**

The earliest visitors to Mana Pools did not have the luxury of looking forward to a cold beer at the end of the day. But thanks to Wilderness Safaris and Ruckomechi Camp, you can now enjoy a chilled lager while some of Africa's most iconic animals congregate near dusk along the mighty Zambezi River.

Mana Pools National Park rests near the northern tip of Zimbabwe at the border with Zambia and encompasses 850 square miles. The namesake pools (mana means "four" in the local Shona language) are ox-bow lakes carved by the Zambezi thousands of years ago as it veered to the north. All serve as havens for a host of species, ranging from aquatic birds to crocodiles and hippo. The Long Pool, which stretches almost four miles, is also is frequented by large herds of elephants that will magically appear from the thick vegetation to seek a bit of refreshment. The region's many ungulates—cape buffalo and impala among them—are also drawn to the water, and this attracts the veldt's predators: lions, leopards, cheetahs, hyenas, and wild dogs. Ruckomechi Camp rests in the heart of the park, along the banks of the Zambezi. Visitors make their homes in spacious tents that face the river, complete with bathrooms and both indoor and outdoor heated showers.

Tendai Mdluli made his way to Mana Pools National Park from the northwestern part of Zimbabwe. "I was born near Lake Chivero Recreational Park," he recalled, "and as a boy, my friends and I did a lot of hunting in the park, shooting birds and such. Sometimes when we were in the park hunting, we'd see the ranger approaching in his jeep. One of us would alert the others—'Game ranger!'—and we'd hide in the culverts or wherever we could. As time went on, I went to school and was educated about why one shouldn't hunt the birds and animals for sport like that. It spurred my interest in becoming a guide. Some years later, after working at a few other safari companies, I joined Wilderness

OPPOSITE: Guests at Wilderness Safaris's Ruckomechi Camp can enjoy a Zambezi lager while watching for game on the nearby Zambezi River at dusk . . . though sometimes the game comes to you.

Safaris and was assigned to Ruckomechi Camp. The first man I met upon coming into camp resembled that game ranger from so many years before. His name is Brian Worsley. I shared my story with him, and he confirmed that he used to operate in that area. We became friends, and he shared much of what he'd learned as a guide."

Guests at Ruckomechi Camp have a number of ways to interact with the wildlife that call Mana Pools home. Game drives (in open Land Rovers) are offered in the early morning and late afternoon, giving visitors the chance to experience a range of habitats. Elephants, elands, buffalo, waterbucks, baboons, zebras, and warthogs are often encountered along the river terraces. "On one drive," Tendai shared, we were close to camp and heard several impalas doing an alarm call. I cut the engine. Moments later, a leopard ran directly in front of our car. We didn't see the kill, but it was clear that it had gotten an impala. We came to the sight of the kill; the impala was so large that the leopard couldn't haul it up into the tree. While we were observing, a pride of lion came along and took the kill for themselves." There's also the option of walking the bush surrounding the camp; the foliage has enough breaks for guests (and their guide) to identify dangerous animals before close encounters can occur. There are also "hides" where guests can wait in the bush for wildlife to appear. "Sometimes, visitors are happy to simply sit on the stargazing deck we have in front of camp, facing the river," Tendai added. "You'll often see water buffalo, elephant, hippo, and crocodiles."

One of Tendai's favorite ways to experience the Mana Pools's wildlife is on the Zambezi itself. "You can navigate the river in a pontoon boat, a speedboat, or a canoe," he described. "The canoe lets you drift silently. If you've never floated past hippos, your heart is on edge. They are very powerful animals and can be dangerous. But our guides know the channels in and out and how to avoid the spots they frequent. Every now and again a hippo will pop out unexpectedly and spray you, which certainly adds to the adventure. Some of our guests may choose to do some fishing. One of the species you can catch is the tigerfish—they grab the bait very hard, and your rod is bent double with the fight. I've caught them to twenty pounds. They are great jumpers; sometimes they'll land in the boat.

"I can't think of a better place in the world to enjoy a cold beer than along the banks of the Zambezi, with the sun setting as the hippos are grunting and the flat plain beyond is teeming with animal life." Tendai's beer of choice is Zambezi lager, a slightly bitter lager that's brewed in Zimbabwe with maize as well as malt and hops. While lagers dominate southern Africa in terms of European beer styles, sorghum beer, such as Chibuku, is also popular. Made with malted sorghum as well as maize (and sometimes millet), sorghum beers like Chibuku are generally low alcohol and have a very limited shelf life.

The pleasures of a frosty beer after a day on the hot, dry Rift Valley can't be overstated. But one travels to Zimbabwe primarily to encounter the region's rich animal life. Sometimes these iconic creatures are encountered from a comfortable distance. And sometimes the animals make it a bit easier, as Tendai recounted: "We had just come back from the evening game drive and had escorted guests to their rooms to freshen up for dinner when we heard an emergency air horn going at close intervals. I quickly grabbed my rifle and flashlight and ran to the rescue. I then saw three lionesses. The moment they saw me approaching, they moved off in a steady pace to a distance of about fifty yards and stopped. I shined my torch at the lions so the guests could see them, reassuring them that they were more than safe in their tents."

TENDAI MDLULI is a senior guide at Wilderness Safaris Ruckomechi Camp and the Trade and Relationship Manager for the Zambezi Region. Before Ruckomechi, Tendai guided in Zimbabwe's renowned Hwange National Park. He holds a professional guiding license. When he's not guiding or hosting guests and agents in camp, Tendai lives in Victoria Falls with his family. He enjoys fishing the Zambezi on his days off.

If You Go

▶ **Getting There:** Guests generally fly to Johannesburg, and then on to Victoria Falls, which is served by several carriers, including British Airways (800-247-9297; www.british airways.com) and South African Airways (800-722-9675; www.flysaa.com). From Victoria Falls, a charter flight delivers you to Wilderness Safaris Ruckomechi Camp.

▶ **Best Time to Visit:** June through October is the best time to visit Mana Pools and Wilderness Safaris Ruckomechi Camp.

▶ **Spots to Visit:** Wilderness Safaris Ruckomechi Camp (+27 11 807 1800; www.wilderness-safaris.com) offers a host of animal viewing opportunities, fishing . . . and the Zambezi lagers are always ice cold.

Library of Congress Control Number: 2016932044

ISBN: 978-1-4197-2216-5

Photograph credits: Page 2: Barry Brecheisen; Page 8: Staatliches Hofbräuhaus in München; Page 12: Allabash Brewing Company; Page 14: Alexandre Ribeiro Dos Santos; Page 17: Cary Norton for Good People Brewing Company; Page 20: Wes Wylie/Tordrillo Mountain Lodge; Page 24: Y Dumoriter/Shutterstock; Page 28: Cookie Bar/Restaurant; Page 32: Christina Karagiannis; Page 36: Peter Bender; Page 42: Brown Cannon III; Page 46: androver/Shutterstock.com; Page 50: The Regents of the University of California, Davis campus 2010; Page 54: Stone Brewing; Page 58: Anchor Brewing Company; Page 62: Sorbis/Shutterstock.com; Page 66: Brewers Association; Page 70: Barry Brecheisen; Page 74: Plzensky Prazdroj, a.s.; Page 78: allou/Shutterstock.com; Page 82: Andreas Ivarsson; Page 86: Andrey Krav/iStock; Page 90: Nikada/iStock; Page 94: Staatliches Hofbräuhaus in München; Page 98: Jim Klug; Page 102: Kat Cannell Photography; Page 106: Goose Island Beer Co.; Page 111: Tania Araujo; Page 114: Kirk Deeter; Page 120: Danita Delimont/Dissolve; Page 126: Briana Jaro; Page 132: Boston Beer Corporation; Page 140: Traverse City Tourism; Page 144: Urban Chestnut Brewing Co.; Page 150: NPS/Jacob W. Frank; Page 154: Tough Mudder, Inc.; Page 158: Berkeley T. Merchant; Page 164: Brooklyn Brewery; Page 160: Wellington Regional Economic Development Agency; Page 172: Jordan Hughes/Wicked Weed Brewing; Page 176: Pete Alport/Visit Bend; Page 180: Michael Peterson; Page 188: Chris Mullins; Page 196: Stephen Finn/Shutterstock.com; Page 200: Ricardo Brazziell/Austin American-Statesman via AP; Page 204: Whit Richardson; Page 208: Bob M. Montgomery Images; Page 212: Bokeh Box Media; Page 216: Lakefront Brewery, Inc.; Page 220: Dana Allen/Wilderness Safaris.

Editor: Samantha Weiner
Designer: Anna Christian
Production Manager: Katie Gaffney

This book was composed in Interstate, Scala, and Village.

Printed and bound in China
10 9 8 7 6 5 4 3 2

Abrams Image books are available at special discounts when purchased in quantity for premiums and promotions as well as fundraising or educational use. Special editions can also be created to specification. For details, contact specialsales@abramsbooks.com or the address below.

ABRAMS The Art of Books
115 West 18th Street
New York, NY 10011
www.abramsbooks.com